All About

Volcanoes and

Earthquakes

By Frederick H. Pough

Former Curator of Physical Geology and Minerals
American Museum of Natural History

Illustrated by Kurt Wiese

RANDOM HOUSE

NEW YORK

NINTH PRINTING

LIBRARY OF CONGRESS CATALOG CARD NUMBER: 53-6282

MANUFACTURED IN THE U.S.A.

Contents

1.

After a Thousand Years

On the Italian mainland near the Bay of Naples there is a fire-breathing mountain. The ancient Romans stood in the greatest awe of it, believing it to be the chimney of Vulcan's forge. "See," they would say as they watched the black smoke rising and the fiery glow playing around the vent, "Vulcan is at his anvil. He is forging thunderbolts for Jupiter, he is beating out weapons for Mars." The exploding sounds from the mountain's depths seemed to them to be the mighty hammer blows of their blacksmith god. *Vulcano* they called the fire-breathing mountain—and gave us the name for all such mountains.

Why the Romans should have decided that this particular volcano was the workshop of their god, nobody can say. But it isn't surprising that they should have fancied such a story. In those days there was no earth science so people had to fill in with imagination what they couldn't fill in with fact. And so far as fire-breathing mountains were concerned, all the Romans knew of them was that they were dangerous. It wasn't wise to get too close when a cloud was coming out of the top. They didn't know that a volcano might seem to be quite dead and then all of a sudden go into action. When after a thousand years and more Vesuvius suddenly woke up, it took them very much by surprise.

A thousand years is a long time. In a thousand years a volcano loses its scars. In a thousand years rain and frost and wind can change its ravaged sides into a green and smiling land. So it was with Vesuvius. Its wounds were healed. In a thousand years its slopes had become covered with fertile farms and fruitful vineyards. Even its burnt crater was green and vine covered. Down near the volcano's foot lay a ring of pleas-

Naples, Italy, with Vesuvius in the background

ant cities. Chief among these were Pompeii, sacred to
Venus, and Herculaneum, the city of Hercules. So
delightful was life in these two that many a famous
Roman had a villa in one or the other. Pompeii especially was renowned for its roses, its wines and its
pleasures.

And then it happened. On August 24, 79 A.D.,
around the hour of noon a great white cloud, shaped
like a gigantic pine tree, rose out of the crater of
Vesuvius. The earth, which had shaken repeatedly for

several days, shook again. There was a rumbling and then an explosion. And before the astonished inhabitants of the towns understood what had happened, the white cloud had turned dark and showers of stones the size of walnuts were sifting down on them.

Panic took hold of the people. Those who were outdoors rushed in; those who were inside rushed out. Had the end of the world come? Had the gods deserted them? No one knew what to do, whether to flee or whether to stay. Wrapping cloaks around their heads or tying cushions on to protect themselves from the falling stones, people ran here and ran there. Now the whole top of the mountain was covered by a black pall of smoky steam. Everything grew dark, and a terrible smell of sulphur filled the air. The earth rocked violently so that buildings were almost wrenched from their foundations. Fires broke out.

"Should we stay or should we go?" In Pompeii everyone was asking this question. Most couldn't make up their minds to forsake their homes and all their belongings. Surely the rain of ashes must come to a stop. For days people stayed in their houses praying to the gods.

And still the pitiless sky continued to bombard them.

Some took food and, herding their children together, went down into the cellars. Others climbed to the upper story to escape the ashes that sifted into the ground floor. Still others finally made up their minds to flee. Seizing whatever had greatest value for them, they hurried through the ash-filled streets to the town gates. Alas! For many it was too late. They had delayed too long. Even as they fled, suffocating fumes from the volcano overwhelmed them. Here a woman with a jewel casket and bottles of precious perfume in her hands sank down never again to rise. There a proud beauty fell gasping for breath with her favorite mirror by her side. The owner of a villa, key in hand, reached his garden gate. His slaves, carrying money and valuables, were close behind. But at the gate, master and slaves were all overcome by the deadly fumes.

And those who stayed were no better off. The gases penetrated everywhere while for eight days and nights the ashes fell. Ashes covered all. Little by little the city with its dead sank from view. Of twenty thousand people in Pompeii perhaps not more than two thousand survived.

From Herculaneum more escaped. For in Herculaneum there could be no dallying, nobody thought of trying to save anything. There what to do was clear-cut. For suddenly down from the mountainside there poured a mighty torrent of liquid mud. The stream of ashes mixed with rain and underground water moved with terrible slowness. But it moved relentlessly. It came straight toward the city. Before that torrent of mud the people fled—toward the sea, out into the countryside, anywhere to get away. Then slowly the mud swept through the streets. It seeped into houses, it filled up the interiors, it covered all. Mud swallowed the city while still the ashes poured from the sky.

Years passed, hundreds and hundreds of years. And men forgot. Where had Pompeii and Herculaneum stood? No one remembered. The very names of the two cities were forgotten.

In the year 1738 a new Queen came to Naples. The young wife of Charles III was from the north. She was enchanted by the sunny gardens of her Italian palace. Most of all she was captivated by the antique statues which here and there adorned the flower beds or stood half hidden in the shrubbery's shade. Where had the statues come from? Could she get some more?

Some, the Queen was told, had been accidentally found on Mt. Vesuvius. Others had been dug from a

Carrying what they could, people hurried to the town gates

site at its foot. About twenty years before this, Prince
Elbeuf, it seemed, had wanted some crushed marble.
Peasants had told him that on the slope of Mt. Vesuvius
there were pits from which they had taken many
statues. Elbeuf had dug down and got out a large
number of them—the shaft was open still.

The Queen lost no time setting diggers to work. Passages were cut out from the open shaft, holes blasted. And at last the rewards came in. Pieces of several huge bronze statues were unearthed. Then three marble statues of Romans in togas appeared. Painted columns and the trunk of a bronze horse came next. Then a flight of stairs was discovered.

By this time the King was as excited about the digging as the Queen. What kind of building was this they were tunneling into?

A few weeks later the answer came. It was a theater. Here was a marker that said so! Somebody named Rufus had built, at his own expense, this "Herculanean Theater." No wonder Elbeuf had found so many statues! The back wall of the theater had been adorned with them. It had collapsed. And Elbeuf had accidentally tunneled into the very middle of the stage, onto which the wall with its statues had fallen.

But what was the meaning of a theater? A theater wouldn't have stood by itself. A theater was always part of a city. A city, then, must lie beneath the mud-cemented ashes through which they were tunneling!

Herculaneum! The word acted like an electric shock. Scholars hunted up old records. They got out the let-

Ruins of Pompeii

ters of the writer Pliny the Younger, who as a seventeen-year-old boy had witnessed the eruption of Vesuvius. They read again how his uncle, Pliny the Elder, naturalist and commander of the fleet, had lost his life trying to rescue folk fleeing from the mountain's fury. Herculaneum! So this was where the city had stood! And where was Pompeii?

People dug. They found the villas and the shops, they found the temples and the bathhouses. They unearthed the paintings on the walls, the statues in the gardens. With growing curiosity, they handled the objects people had used daily in their houses, work-shops and inns. Everything was there, miraculously preserved for sixteen and a half centuries.

They found the dead. In an upper room at Pompeii a family of eleven had died together. In the cellars of a noble villa eighteen women and children lay with their heads covered as though asleep. Near a garden gate a group of men had been entombed together with bags of money and valuables they had tried to carry away. One held a key in his hand. A woman with a ring on her finger, pendants in her ears, and slippers on her dainty feet lay on her back. Only an amber cupid and a mirror lay by her side.

Mt. Lassen

2.

How Does a Volcano Work?

What are these fire-breathing mountains that can wake up after a thousand years and bury whole cities from sight?

We call them mountains—Mt. Vesuvius, we say, Mt. Etna, Mt. Pelée, Mt. Lassen, Mt. Hekla. But volcanoes are not ordinary mountains. They are not formed by folding and crumpling. They are not made by uplifting and weathering. Volcanic mountains are an outpouring of hot materials from deep inside the earth. Volcanic mountains are built of the stone that has come out of their own centers. Sometimes that stone explodes out in the form of cinders. More often the rock comes up as a red-hot liquid that we call *lava*.

By latest count there are some 500 active volcanoes in the world. But, as everyone knows, they aren't to be found everywhere. In the whole of the United States there is only one active one. Volcanoes spring up only in special places. For they are just sores, blisters on the earth's crust. They break out only where the crust is weak, only where it springs a leak.

Are we, then, to suppose that down under the crust of the earth the rock is in a liquid state? Are we to suppose that it lies there waiting for a chance to squeeze out?

We cannot see through the earth's crust. We can't be sure what is going on far below. The deepest hole we have ever dug is only four miles down to the bottom, and that's just a scratch in the earth's skin. The deepest mine is half that deep. To be sure, mountains wear away and show us rocks that once lay five or more miles beneath those vanished mountains. Also, valleys are weathered deep in rocks that were pushed high up into the air. Having seen so much of the earth

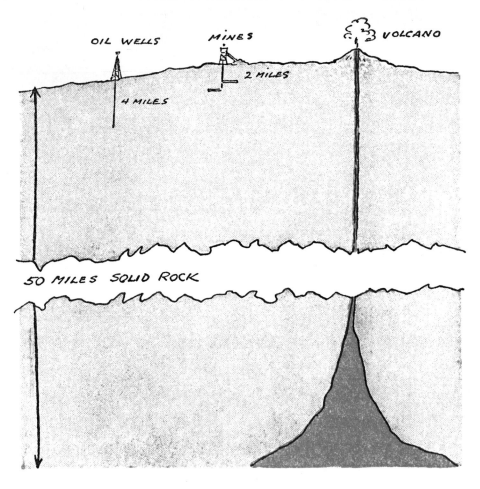

OIL WELLS   MINES   VOLCANO

2 MILES

4 MILES

50 MILES SOLID ROCK

exposed, we can say we know what the crust is like for the first five or six miles down. What lies below?

Well, we can make a guess that the next forty-five miles are pretty much like the lowest rocks we have seen on top. We can be fairly sure that for about fifty miles the earth is solid. And we can be sure of something else, too. Though the rocks of the crust are solid, they aren't of the same temperature. Every mile down they are a little hotter. Near the bottom of the crust they must be pretty hot, hot enough to glow. We know that because we have learned a thing or two from mines and tunnels and deep wells. We have learned that the farther down we go, the hotter it gets. Our deepest mine has to be air-conditioned. At the rate the temperature increases as we go down, perhaps thirty or forty miles down the temperature is as high as 2,000 degrees!

How, then, can we suppose rock fifty miles down to be solid?

Time was, and not so long ago, when scientists believed this rock was not solid. They were certain that below the crust the interior of the earth must be liquid. Didn't the boiling hot lava pouring out of volcanoes prove that? Could the rock under the earth's crust be anything but liquid, seeing how hot it must be down there?

Scientists don't believe that any more. The seismograph—the instrument which records earthquake shocks —has changed their ideas about the inside of the earth. The seismograph shows that some of the shock waves pass through the first 1,800 miles of the earth as though

it were rigid. They do not pass the way they do through a liquid but the way they pass through a steel ball. That seems to settle the question. The rocks under the crust of the earth can't be liquid. They are hot enough to melt certainly. But they don't melt.

Why? Because they have no room to melt in. The crust of the earth by its tremendous weight seals them in. In order to melt, the hot rocks would have to expand. And the fifty or sixty miles of cooler layers above hold them down so tightly that they can't expand. So there they stay—hot enough to melt, yet unable to do so.

But how, then, can we account for lava? Surely that's liquid rock coming from inside the earth!

It isn't easy to account for lava. It may be that somewhere, for some reason, the weight of the crust lessens. Maybe the crust is squeezed and arched up a little—perhaps because the inside of the earth has shrunk a bit and the crust wrinkles. That would relieve the pressure and let the hot rocks fifty miles down expand so they become liquid. Or it may be that for some reason the rocks in some region of the crust have become especially hot. Maybe radioactive elements are behind lava. We have learned recently that certain elements break down and change into other substances. When they do that, they give off heat. If that heat doesn't escape through the earth's crust as fast as it forms, the rocks in that place must get steadily hotter. In time they might get hot enough to melt in spite of the pressure of the solid crust above.

When all is said, though, we have to admit that we don't know exactly what causes volcanoes. We can't be sure what gives the rocks a chance to melt. We know that in some places there is molten rock—or *magma*, as lava is called when it is under the crust. But we can only guess at the forces that combine to make it.

Nor can we be sure what makes the lava rise. We know that lava breaks through in the weak places of the crust, places where there is some sort of crack. But heat alone isn't enough to make lava come up. Something else is needed. Perhaps that something else is gas.

It may be that lava acts the same way as soda water in a bottle. Everyone has seen bubbles come out of soda and rush to the top of the bottle when the cap is removed. Little bubbles start coming up from the bottom. They grow bigger and bigger on the way up. As they come up to the top and break, they may splash a little soda out of the bottle.

Perhaps the gas in lava behaves like that. We know there is lots of gas in lava. Most of the volcano's fireworks are caused by gas. The explosions that throw rocks out of volcanic craters result from the bubbling of gas out of lava. There is so much gas in lava that all of it doesn't escape at once. As the lava flows out, it keeps on bubbling quietly. And even after it stops flowing, it may keep steaming for months.

Surely all this gas must have something to do with making the lava come up. But gas alone wouldn't do it. Gas can't be the only thing. The weak place in the crust must be there first to make it easier for the lava to rise. Given the weak place, we can assume that gas helps the lava to eat its way up.

Perhaps that's how fire-breathing mountains work.

3.

A Volcano Is Born

It isn't often that people have the chance to see a volcano born. When it happens, it is a world event; for nothing in Nature is more spectacular. That's why in 1943 the papers were full of Parícutin, the little Mexican volcano born in a corn field.

The corn field belonged to an Indian named Dionisio Polido. It was a good field even though there was one low place where the corn never grew very well. Dionisio always plowed and planted that spot anyway. Who knew? Perhaps some day he would get as good a crop from the low place as anywhere else.

One afternoon in February, 1943, Dionisio was out with his oxen, plowing his field. The sun was unusually hot that day, and the ground felt strangely warm to his bare feet—particularly in the low place. The furrows he was turning seemed endlessly long. As he guided his plow, the Indian smoked a home-made cigarette. Somehow it shortened the rows to smoke.

Once as he turned his ox team to come back across the field, Dionisio thought he saw smoke rising from the low place. How was that? Was the stub of his last cigarette still burning? It might set some dead corn-stalks on fire. This was the dry season—the fire might spread. Leaving his team, Dionisio went over to see. Yet even as he walked it seemed to him there was too much smoke for just one cigarette. And, indeed, as he leaned over to look, his sombrero fell beside a smoking crack in the ground. Dionisio stood staring at it puzzled. What could be burning there?

All of a sudden a rumbling noise rose from deep down in the earth. At the same time the ground shook—harder than any earthquake Dionisio had ever felt. It

swayed so that he could hardly stand. Then with a
roar a new and larger crevice opened in the ground
beside his sombrero, and to his amazement Dionisio
saw his straw hat fly high into the air. Before it hit
the ground again, he was running for help. He turned
only once. From the place where the smoke rose, a
fountain of stones was shooting. It looked as if someone inside the earth were throwing rocks into the air.

Dionisio didn't stop to watch. Never had his legs
carried him so fast as now, making for the priest's
house in San Juan, three miles away.

In San Juan everybody already knew that something unusual was happening. For even at this distance the rumbling could clearly be heard. And now while excited Dionisio poured out his story, a whole series of explosions blasted the air. In the distance a thin column of smoke could be seen climbing into the sky.

"I will go with you, my son," the priest said quickly. A handful of the braver men volunteered to go along. As they passed through Parícutin, the village near the corn field, more folk joined them.

They had need of all their courage, for Dionisio's corn field presented a terrifying sight. On the spot where the low place had always been, stood a smoking pile of black rubble. It was tall as a tree. From its center a steady stream of rocks shot high into the air. And as they fell, they piled up around the opening, building a chimney for the column of black smoke that steadily belched forth.

The people stood on the edge of the corn field crossing themselves and moving their lips in silent prayer. "It is a volcano!" the priest said at last in an awed voice. "It is a volcano being born!"

"Yes, yes, it is a volcano!" the people echoed. They knew volcanoes. There were many in the nearby

region, and though none had erupted in their time, all
the Indians recognized the shape it was taking on. By
now the pile of rocks looked like a gigantic upside-
down ice cream cone. Only a volcano would build a
cone like that.

It was frightening to hear the explosions increase
from moment to moment. It was frightening to see the
glowing hot rocks shoot up into the sky, curve out-
ward, then fall among the old stalks in the corn field
or back upon the cone.

With darkness the spectacle became even more terrifying. The wider the cone grew, the more bombs fell on the slope itself. In the dark they glowed like giant coals so that the whole pile was outlined in fire. From its center a burning torch of red fragments rose into the sky. What would happen next? How high would the cone get? All through the night the people watched.

In the morning they saw the cone was two hundred feet high! But the pile no longer glowed—the stones that had built it were black as coal.

And now from far and near folk came streaming up to see the wonder. Cars jammed the dirt road that wound from Parícutin around Dionisio's corn field. Terrifying as the sights and sounds were, everybody held himself lucky to be in on the birth of a volcano. It was something to tell one's grandchildren about.

So far no melted rock had leaked out. There were big rocks—bombs—and many smaller bits of stone, but not till a week had passed did any lava make its appearance. At first it was a stiff, doughy mass that squeezed from an opening at the side of the cone. The outside of the lava was so cool that it was black, but as the doughy inside pushed on the brittle crust, it

cracked and pieces of the stone fell off. Then for a while a red glow showed in the crevice in the rock pile. And again the crust would blacken—till the next thrust of the doughy inside broke off a piece. It was as if a giant were pushing forward an endless pile of loose, hot rocks.

The first flow of lava went only a few hundred yards and stopped. Along the motionless front, steam and white clouds of vapor poured out from a hundred crevices. White, salty-tasting crusts formed on the rocks wherever steam came out. Then a second tongue of lava broke through alongside the first. It was a little hotter than the first and went a little farther. No sooner had it stopped than another flow broke out, and after it others. Each seemed a little hotter, each went a little farther. Finally Dionisio's corn field disappeared altogether. And the lava flows spilled on—out into the forest around the field.

Meantime the fireworks kept going. At times the bombs that shot from the volcano's throat flew 3,000 feet into the air before they started to fall. Flashes of lightning played in the ash column that rose from the crater. The ground shook in constant earthquakes. And always the lava gushed. Dionisio's field now lay under 300 feet of stone. The cone that rose above the lava was more than a quarter of a mile high. Its base measured a mile across. People named the volcano Parícutin after the neighboring village. The village of Parícutin was soon to die because the ash that constantly filled the air made life impossible.

Scientists from great distances had come to study the new volcano. None of them had been there from the beginning. So all were delighted when Parícutin started up in a new place—just the way it had the first time when only Dionisio had been there to see. Near the bottom of the cone a little crack opened in the top of a lava flow. A few rocks shot out. Then the crack grew bigger. In a few days there sat a baby volcano, spitting out rocks just like Parícutin. *Zapicho*, "Little Son," the Indians called the baby.

Zapicho filled the air with a steady stream of little stones. But Parícutin, meantime, had slowed down because gas that should have come out of the big cone was leaking away through the little one. The Indians hoped it was a sign the volcano was dying. "It will soon stop now," they kept saying. "It will stop." Instead, at the end of a couple of months it was Zapicho that died.

And no sooner did that happen than the big volcano started up again. At the same time another crack opened on its other side and red-hot lava began to pour out. It flowed and flowed. It flowed endlessly. A million tons and more a day came out for months and months. A solid crust formed over the lava like a roof. You could walk over it and not know there was red-hot lava underneath. Only when the roof cracked was there a sign of how hot it was inside. It was dangerous to step on an open crack because the invisible hot gas underneath would burn up your shoe.

The lava spread and spread until at last a tongue reached out and covered the village that had given the volcano its name. Was the lava going to swallow San

Juan, as it had swallowed the town of Parícutin?

In spite of the threat, the people of San Juan still clung to their town. All the trees in the surrounding forests were dead or dying. Corn patches were buried in gray dust. There was no longer grass for horses or cows or oxen. The women no longer had time for the embroidery that once had made their village famous. They were too busy fighting the dust. Nor could the men work in the dead forest. They spent their time shoveling ash that blocked the streets and weighed down roofs till it threatened to wreck the houses. The San Juan folk knew their town was doomed, but still they hoped against hope. Perhaps Parícutin would spare them. Though a new site had been chosen, streets laid out, fields cleared, the people couldn't bring themselves to leave.

But at last they had to. A new lava flow had started out and was moving straight toward San Juan. It came down through the woods; it filled the valley leading to the town. In a great hurry everything that could be moved had to be piled on trucks. Doorways and window frames and boards came down. Statues and pictures, benches and old carved doors were carried from the church. Men climbed into the tower and lowered the big bronze bells.

A few months later only the towers of the old church and a wall or two, missed by the lava, remained.

But with San Juan's destruction, Parícutin had reached almost the end of its powers. On March 1, 1952, the last bit of stone exploded. A few days later the lava stopped leaking. Parícutin was dead.

The volcano had run its course in only a little over

nine years. In those nine years it had built a cone 1,600 feet high. It had covered 100 square miles with thick ash deposits. It had leaked millions of tons of lava that in many places lay 300 feet deep. And it had taught scientists more than they could have learned from watching the occasional flows of a dozen great volcanoes. Little Parícutin had had its good side as well as its bad.

4.

They Aren't All Alike

Parícutin is a cinder cone, and its life was probably in no way different from that of thousands of other cinder cones the world over. We know a good deal about such volcanoes now. They are the commonest kind. Whenever we see in the papers that a new volcano has appeared somewhere, it is almost sure to turn out to be another cinder cone. That has happened several times in this country. We know that the eruptions of such volcanoes don't last very long. And we know that when they finally stop, they don't start up again.

Out in Arizona we have an almost perfect cinder cone, a beautiful little volcano. It is very tempting to climb the few hundred yards up to Sunset Crater's top. But it's not easy. You slide back a foot for every thirteen inches you climb. For its sides are nothing but loose, gray gravel. You don't need to know much about volcanoes to recognize Sunset Crater as a very fresh one. It looks as if it might have erupted only a few years ago. And, indeed, the Indians have a legend about the time when it was active. But that probably was before any white man found his way to the West.

Little volcanoes like Sunset Crater all look like piles of loose cinders. That's why they are known as cinder cones. In some parts of the world there are a great many of them. A few will look as fresh and as recent as Sunset Crater. Others right near by will show their age by the trees that cover their sides and the deep gullies that groove them. Here and there among the cinder cones will be big mountains made of lava as well as loose cinders.

That makes the scientists wonder. Were all these big volcanoes cinder cones at one time? If a cinder cone

kept erupting long enough, would it turn into a big volcano? It is hard to know. No one has ever seen a cinder cone turn into a big volcano.

Cinder cones can be found in almost all recent volcanic regions. They seem to mark places where a small lava pocket has eaten its way to the top. Probably the lava in such small pockets has lots of gas in it and that's the reason why cinder cones are so explosive. The gas in the lava blows out violently. It throws the lava high up in the air. Much gets shredded into pretty small bits and comes down in a shower of solid stone to pile up around the opening of the volcano.

Some cinder cones don't produce any lava flows at all. Others do. But a flow from a cinder cone doesn't come out at the top. As scientists learned by watching Parícutin, the lava is likely to flow out at the side. After all, a cinder cone is only a pile of loose rocks— it isn't strong enough to hold up a pool of lava. For lava is a liquid. Like any liquid, as soon as it pushes up out of a hole in the ground, it wants to spread out. If there is a small cinder cone in its path, it just pushes out the lowest side and carries it away.

Of all volcanoes, cinder cones do the least harm. They don't remain active for long. The recent ones we know about seem to erupt for only a few years, or a few months or weeks, and then stop. The whole cone is built up in that time. Generally these volcanoes can't grow more than 1,000 or 1,500 feet in the time they have. Parícutin, as we saw, did a little better than that.

How do we explain cinder cones? Why do they live so short a time?

We can't explain them any better than we can the big volcanoes. But one thing is certain: cinder cones and big volcanoes are all part of one process because we find them right in the same region. Some volcanic regions are dotted with little cinder cones. Small pockets of lava work their way to the surface, first in one place, then years later in another. This goes on for hundreds and hundreds of years. The cones may be many miles apart or they may be very close together. We cannot guess where or when the next one will appear.

A big cone volcano naturally takes much longer to build up. Many centuries go into its making. But it acts pretty much the same way as a cinder cone though on a larger scale. There is one big difference. When a cinder cone stops erupting, it's through. But a big volcano can rest for a thousand years and start up again. It must be that the lava of a big volcano eats a very big channel up through the crust. Unlike the feeding tube of a cinder cone, the channel doesn't freeze solid all the way down after the volcano stops erupting. Not, at least, until it's really dead.

In a big cone volcano the lava spills over the top. In part, that happens because the lava has less gas in it when it comes up in the crater and so is less frothy and explosive. But in part, also, it is because the cone is stronger. The big volcano cone is not a pile of loose rocks. It was built by flow after flow of lava. It is solid stone so it can hold up a pool of lava very well.

After many years an old, sleeping volcano looks like a quiet, peaceful mountain. Trees grow in its crater, vines cover its top. The slopes often have soil where coffee or grapes grow exceptionally well. People think of the volcano as their friend. It hasn't erupted in so long that they suppose it to be dead. Busy towns spring up at its foot. Then one day the giant may wake up. Homes start to shake. Rumbles come from the ground. A crevice may open and steam drift out.

Then it is high time to move. For the volcano may come back to life with an explosion that will ruin the country for miles around. History tells of many eruptions as destructive as that of Vesuvius in 79 A.D. And there will be many more in the years to come.

It is easy enough to recognize a volcano like the Japanese Fujiyama. It has a huge cone as perfect as Sunset Crater. But there are volcanoes on our earth that don't build up a very cone-like shape. We call them shield or dome-shaped volcanoes. The molten stone that builds them has only a little gas in it; so instead of exploding with violence, their lava escapes quietly and flows rapidly away. That's why it doesn't build a cone. Naturally it takes a long time to build a

Diamond Head, Honolulu

high dome. Think how long it must have taken to build the Hawaiian Islands, which are the best examples of dome volcanoes that we have!

The eruptions of dome volcanoes aren't very dangerous. As there are no violent explosions, little harm can be done. The only dangerous part is the rapidly flowing lava, but very few people have ever been caught by it. Yet dome volcanoes aren't so friendly to man as the big cones. The slopes of the domes are likely to be largely bare rock because their watery lava leaves a smooth surface that takes a very long time to weather into soil. Nor is the soil especially good anyway since there isn't much plant food in that kind of lava.

Very fluid lava doesn't always make dome volcanoes. Sometimes it builds no volcano at all. The lava comes up out of cracks in the crust in sheets and spreads flat and far. In time, as flow follows flow, a great plateau can build up.

We've not seen many eruptions from cracks, or fissure eruptions. In modern times the greatest one occurred about 200 years ago in Iceland. Vast quantities of lava poured then from 22 openings along a line 10 miles long. The lava flowed into the channel of a river, causing great floods in which about 9,000 people and 230,000 horses and cows perished. But for the most part fissure flows happened long ago. And they happened on a much grander scale. In Washingon and Oregon and Idaho the lava spread out like a sea hundreds of feet thick. It covered an area bigger than all New England. In India and southern Brazil and Uruguay it built great plateaus.

Lava plateaus take a long time to build, and perhaps thousands of years pass between flows. Maybe high lava plains are still forming on the earth, and we don't recognize it because they take so long to form. Maybe the Iceland flow was one of a whole series. Maybe lava will build a great plain there some day.

Crater Lake

There is much about eruptions we don't know. The volcano we call a *caldera* is all a mystery to us. We can only guess at the way it is formed; for we have never seen one in the making. It is a volcano within a volcano! The moon has craters like that—craters with little cones scattered on their floor. Here in the United States we have only one caldera—Crater Lake. The sides of that volcano are like those of a very large mountain, but the top is chopped off flat. Instead of a peak there is a great hole filled with water, above which an island shows.

Scientists used to think the top of the caldera must have been blown off in one terrific explosion. But there just isn't enough loose rock lying around to fit in with such a theory. Now we think that one time as the gas rushed to get out, it took almost all the lava in the pocket with it, leaving a great empty hole under the mountain. The weight of the peak got to be too much, and the top collapsed into the hole. Then the last of the gas and the lava worked their way out through the broken-up mountain and made a little cinder cone. That's Wizard Island in Crater Lake.

No calderas have formed in historical times, but we can't be certain they are things of the past. For volcanic activity surely isn't dying out. It may seem so to us because all around us we see old volcanic rocks in places where there isn't a trace of a volcano today. "How much more vulcanism there used to be!" we think. But probably that's a mistake. Probably there are as many eruptions now in one year as there ever were since the crust became really solid and thick.

5.

The Pacific Ring of Fire

Somewhere in the world a volcano is erupting all the time. We keep reading about it in the papers. Now it's here, now it's there. But of one thing you can be pretty sure: it is probably not anywhere near by. In the United States we don't have a lot of volcanoes that are likely to go off. The last time it happened was back in 1915 when a mountain in California blew up. That was Mt. Lassen, generally considered our only active volcano.

Why are we so especially favored? It hasn't always been that way. There is volcanic rock all around us. We recognize it easily, for rock that came up out of the earth as lava is very different from other rock. Many of our volcanoes have lost their craters, and some don't look much like volcanoes any more. But we recognize them just the same. In the side of a really old volcano where a valley has been worn down through several layers of rock we can see a lot of flows, one on top of another, all sloping away from the top. That tells the story.

As we look around, moreover, we notice that much of the volcanic rock is in places many miles from anything that looks like a volcano today. It strikes us as strange. Yet we find that in a number of other countries it's the same way. Both France and Germany, for instance, have large volcanic areas and no recent volcanoes. What is the reason for this?

We can draw only one conclusion: centers of volcanic activity move around in the earth's crust. Today's centers of vulcanism are different from those of a few million years ago.

Well, where are the present-day centers? Let us dot the 500 or so active volcanoes on the map and see.

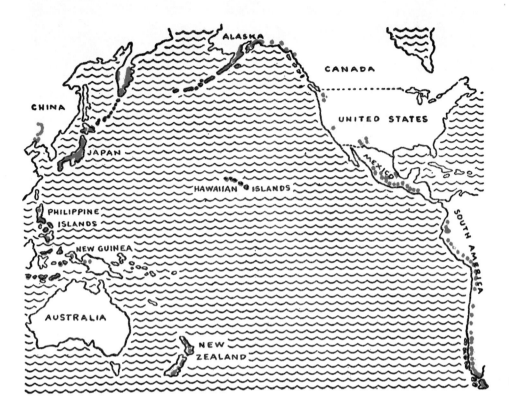

At once a curious pattern shows up. We find that
well over half our dots are somewhere near the Pacific
Ocean. A big row almost surrounds the Pacific like a
belt. The belt isn't perfect. There are stretches along
the shore where there are no volcanoes. Yet on the
whole it is easy to see that all are part of one chain
even if a few links are missing. The rest of the volcanoes are scattered, but they are seldom alone. They
show up in clusters or strings. Some are islands in the
Pacific. Some are near the Mediterranean. Some are
in the center of Africa.

We don't know why the pattern is like that. It has something to do with the cause of volcanoes, and we don't know what that is either. Looking at the row of volcanoes around the Pacific Ocean, some scientists have concluded that the continents are sliding over into the Pacific. That would make a crack in the crust all around the ocean basin and make it easier for the gases and lava to work their way up to the surface.

Sliding over? But do continents slide?

Some time ago an Austrian scientist by the name of Alfred Wegener was looking at the map of the world. He was suddenly struck by a curious thing—something others had noticed before him. The east coast of South America had an outline that would fit into the outline of the west coast of Africa very much like a jigsaw puzzle. Had these two continents once been joined? Had they broken apart and slid away from each other? His eye went further. In his imagination he saw the Atlantic Ocean much narrower and North America 'way over near Europe. Perhaps, he thought, that's how the Atlantic came into being—when the New World cracked off and slid away from the Old.

Over on the other side of Africa, Arabia looked as if it had cracked off and had all but broken away.

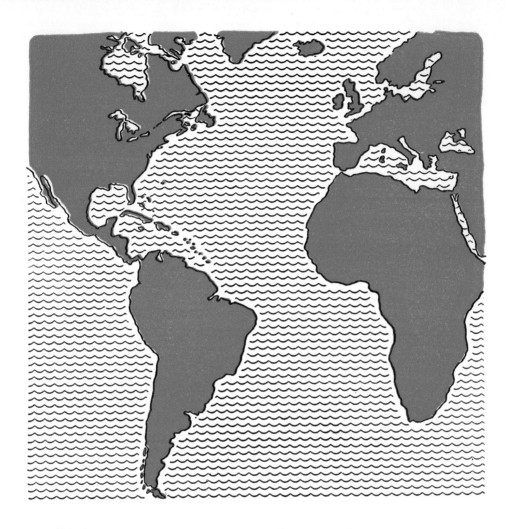

Had India and Australia done the same thing? Wegener studied and studied the map. The more he looked at it, the more he got to thinking that the crust of the earth doesn't stand still. He didn't think of it as floating over a liquid surface but as sliding around on a plastic rock base.

Such a theory is very tempting. It would account not only for the volcanoes but also for the chain of mountains all along the western coast of the two Americas. The rock that makes the ocean basins is basalt. This volcanic rock is much heavier than the rocks that make up the continents. As the continents push against the ocean floor, their edges would bend and crumple, thickening into mountains. And as they crumpled, the crust would be weakened and break in many places, making it easy for the lava to come through and make volcanoes.

Let us take a quick look at the Ring of Fire around the Pacific or what scientists call the Circum-Pacific Volcano Belt. We'll start on the west side of South America.

A whole row of volcanoes dots the Andes Mountains, which follow the western edge of that continent. Some are the highest volcanoes in the world. Chimborazo in Ecuador is the highest of all—over 20,000 feet. It is a dead volcano. Cotopaxi, also in Ecuador, is a thousand feet lower and considered active.

At the top of South America we come to a gap in the chain. And it's a good thing we do because that's where the Panama Canal is. North of the canal, Central America begins to widen, but the volcanoes cling to the west coast. Mexico gets much wider, and there

the volcanoes spread across the country. There is almost a row of volcanoes cutting across the Pacific chain. Parícutin lies in that row. So does Orizaba, the highest mountain in Mexico. West of it, near Mexico City, there are two big volcanoes. One is dead. The other, Popocatepetl, is fresh-looking and may still be active. Almost any morning you can see a little haze coming out of it.

In northern Mexico the belt is broken again, but picks up in Arizona and New Mexico. The volcanoes here are pretty far from the Pacific, and none has erupted since white men have lived in America, though some of the cones look very fresh. Mt. Lassen is active on the west coast. Mt. Hood and Mt. Rainier may still be active. Though these two don't look very active, it still isn't safe to call them surely dead; for there are warm places in them which show that all the heat hasn't escaped yet. Mountains have looked colder than this and have still come back to life.

The North American part of the belt is the poorest of all. In Canada there is another gap, and we don't come to a lot of volcanoes again until we get to Alaska. There a whole string of them starts. In the Aleutian Islands there are several calderas, some with inner cones that erupt quite often. Up in the far north a lot of the volcanoes probably start and finish without anyone ever seeing them erupt because they are so far from any place where people live.

Some of the islands off Alaska are entirely volcanic. There is one that is known as a disappearing island. Bogosloff Island in the Bering Sea has been "discovered" several times; for it has washed away and erupted over and over again.

In the next section of the chain fireworks are pretty frequent. The volcanoes start in Kamchatka, which juts out into the ocean from Siberia, then pass through islands to Japan.

Japan is full of volcanoes, and there have been many terrible disasters. But the Japanese are fond of them just the same, especially Fujiyama, which is said to be the most beautiful volcano in the world.

Down in the Philippines another string of volcanoes starts. Lovely Mt. Mayon, the "Fujiyama of the Philippines," has often erupted. Taal, a little volcano on an island on a lake in the Philippines, is the dangerous kind. When it erupts, it shoots out a heavy cloud of gas and hot, black ashes.

Farther south, in New Guinea, volcanoes are forever causing trouble. There the islands are so thickly settled that there is always a village near any volcano that erupts.

Java and Sumatra are in a bad way, too. They are as full of volcanoes as Japan. They have so many that the Dutch established a volcano observatory there to study eruptions and learn the warning signs.

Krakatoa was once a volcano of this link of the Pacific chain. It was a wooded island lying in the channel between Java and Sumatra, but in 1883 it blew up and almost disappeared.

The East Indies bring us to the end of the Pacific Belt. And it is just here, off the end of Java, that we find one of the deepest places in the ocean. It is as if the crust were bent down here at the end of the line of weak places. The chances are that some day there will be more islands here. New volcanoes may spring up. But it will be millions of years from now. It takes only moments for an island to blow up and disappear; it takes ages to build one up from the bottom.

The Pacific Ring of Fire reveals the weak spots in the earth's crust around the great Pacific basin. But the basin itself is cracked, too. There are whole chains of volcanic islands in the great ocean. Iwo Jima and many other famous islands whose names Americans learned during the second World War are volcanic. There are volcanic islands from New Zealand all the way north to Hawaii, where volcanoes have piled up lava until they have built the highest pile of rocks in the world. One volcano in the Hawaiian Islands reaches nearly 14,000 feet above the sea. But from where it starts on the floor of the Pacific Ocean it is nearly 30,000 feet high, the highest mountain on earth.

And finally there are the countless coral islands. All of them have a volcanic base, for corals can't live more than 100 feet down. They have to start building on ready-made platforms. So every little atoll in the Pacific is a flag. Every colorful reef tells the tale of lava underneath, of a weak spot in the mighty ocean's floor.

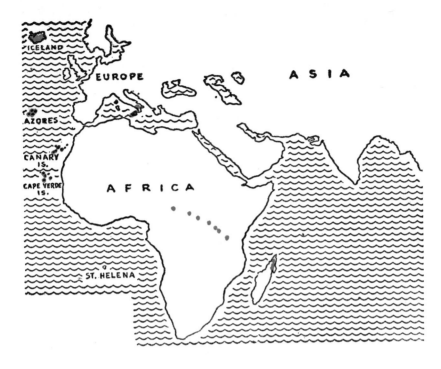

6.

More Weak Spots

Not all the volcanic islands are in the Pacific. As we have already seen, Iceland is made of lava and so are St. Helena, the island to which Napoleon was exiled, and Ascension. The Azores and the Canary Islands and the Cape Verde Islands are volcanic. Bermuda sits on top of a volcano. The West Indies have plenty of volcanoes.

'Way over on the other side of the Atlantic there's another string. Mt. Vesuvius is the only active volcano on the mainland of Europe, but the Mediterranean has a lot. Mt. Etna in Sicily is the largest and highest. It measures 87 miles around the base. Stromboli, on an island just north, erupts all the time. Every night it shines with a red light. Pilots call it "the lighthouse of the Mediterranean" because they can guide their boats by it. The chimney of Vulcan's forge is near by.

East of the Mediterranean we come to another group which includes Mt. Ararat.

The last important cluster of volcanoes lies in the middle of Africa. And here we can actually see that this is one of the weak spots in the earth's crust; for all around are places where it has cracked. Land levels have moved up and down. We can see places where the surface of the earth has dropped as much as 6,000 feet. That's well over a mile!

Usually such cracks are hidden under the ocean, but here the rifts are exposed. The sunken places make long, narrow valleys. These rift valleys of Africa are quite different from ordinary valleys made by running water. The rift valleys drop straight down with very steep walls.

In Central Africa another set of cracks crosses the rifts. So it doesn't surprise us to find that right here is

Mt. Kilimanjaro

a whole row of volcanoes. They straddle the crossing tracks. In Tanganyika lava has piled up the highest mountain in all Africa—Mt. Kilimanjaro. It is near the blazing equator, yet the volcano's crater is so high up in the air that the snow never melts away from its top.

Some of the African volcanoes have very thin and watery lava which flows very fast. One lava flow

recently ran so fast that it almost caught a scientist who was studying it. With two native helpers he found himself walled in between the jungle and the advancing lava. The men couldn't chop their way fast enough to keep ahead of it. If they hadn't come to an open elephant trail just as the lava caught up with them, all of them would have been killed.

Well, such are the present-day centers of vulcanism. We have taken a quick look around at the earth's danger spots, and now we know why we in the United States are especially favored. As we have seen,

volcanoes are erupting only where there are weak places in the earth's crust. And except for our West Coast, we are far from any such. We don't have to be afraid that a volcano will start up in our backyard as it did in Dionisio Polido's corn field. Dionisio, remember, lived in an area of volcanoes.

For millions of years to come it is only in such regions that volcanoes will be born. In Europe we can look for new volcanoes only along the Mediterranean. In Africa we can expect them only in the central part. In Australia there isn't a chance of one starting up at all.

All About Volcanoes and Earthquakes

But even if we live near a volcano, we don't have to worry. For volcanoes give warnings, and if we listen to them and start to leave at once, we'll be all right. We know now that the dangerous volcanoes are the ones that seem to be dead. We are learning what the warnings are. We know that earthquakes and volcanoes go together and that when the earth shakes it is smart to look at the volcano and see what it's doing. If a white cloud starts to come out, it's time to move. We've found out it's better to be safe than sorry, better to go and later find out it wasn't necessary than wait too long. When a cloud of gas and black ash is rushing down from a cone, it's too late to start for safety.

7.

Hurricane Blasts

We say that a volcano is dead if it never has a cloud coming out of its crater, but that word *never* is tricky. Is it 100 years? Five hundred? A thousand? We can't say. Once in a while we put a volcano on the dead list and then have to take it off. We may be mistaken about a lot of volcanoes we call dead.

But, now, what is this white cloud that tells us a volcano is alive and perhaps getting ready to erupt? Is it a gas of some kind?

All About Volcanoes and Earthquakes

Lava, as we have seen, has lots of gas in it. Some of it is carbon dioxide, some is chlorine and fluorine and ammonium chloride and sulphur dioxide. But though a number of these gases have a smell, and a pretty bad one too, they can't be seen. Gases, then, have to be ruled out. They can't account for the cloud. Is it, perhaps, steam?

Yes, water comes out of the earth at a volcano as well as gases. Some of the water comes out in the form of steam. Over the steam a white cloud may form.

But what about the black cloud that looks like smoke?

There isn't any real smoke. Newspapers tell about smoke and flame coming out of a volcano. But how could there be any? What would be burning? When a fire burns, it is burning up something like wood or coal. There isn't anything like that in the rocks that come out of a volcano. The smoke and flame that people think they see above a volcano are just rock dust and red-hot lava. Scientists call the rock dust *ash*. That's unfortunate because it gives people the idea that something is burning.

Although nothing is burning in a volcano, what comes out is frightfully hot. The worst disasters have

been due to the terribly hot gases that explode out
when a dead volcano comes to life. In 1951 a tremendous eruption like that occurred in New Guinea when
Mt. Lamington killed 2,000 people. Not many of us
heard about Mt. Lamington exploding because there
are so many exciting things happening these days that
erupting volcanoes don't get much space in the papers.

Mt. Lamington stands 80 miles northeast of Port
Moresby and looks down on a trail that American
soldiers used when they crossed the island in World

War II. It is an old volcano. Everybody knew it was a volcano, but people thought it was dead and harmless. Certainly nothing about Mt. Lamington gave a hint that something was going on inside. When our soldiers saw it, it was a high, tree-covered mountain no different from any other. The idea that any trouble could come from that source never crossed their minds.

But late in 1950 people suddenly realized that Mt. Lamington wasn't as dead as they thought. Quake after quake shook the earth. After that the astonished inhabitants beheld a thin column of steam drifting out of the volcano. Was it possible that it was going to erupt? People in this region had had no experience of dead volcanoes coming to life. They couldn't believe their own peaceful Mt. Lamington was getting ready for fireworks. But when the earth shook harder and more steam came out, some concluded the volcano really meant business. Quite a number decided to take no chances. They left, bag and baggage. But many stayed because they had no place to go.

Days passed. The earth kept rumbling and shaking. Pretty soon the quakes were so strong that, looking back now, it seems unbelievable all the inhabitants didn't take warnings and go. But even some Europeans,

who certainly should have understood the danger, stayed on.

On the morning of January 21st, a plane was passing some miles off on its way to Port Moresby. All of a sudden the passengers were startled to see a huge cloud of smoke leap up from the mountain and mushroom skyward. The pilot at once turned the plane around. He wanted to investigate what was going on. But fifteen miles from the smoke edge the plane began to bump about so in the disturbed air currents that he changed his mind. Thinking of the passengers' safety, he turned again and flew away from the area.

This was the first and main eruption. Within minutes, hundreds of square miles of the mountain were smothered under a cloud of volcanic ash. The atmosphere was so thick with ash all around that even next morning rescue planes couldn't land. They couldn't find the landing field on account of the blackness. Yet that field was nineteen miles from Mt. Lamington.

Higatura, ten miles from the volcano, was wiped out. From Sangara, a mile farther off, a few persons escaped. But it was only by a miracle. As the dense wall of jet-black, burning-hot smoke was rushing down the mountain toward them, a sudden gust of wind came up. For three minutes—so the survivors said—it held the cloud back. It gave them just time enough to pile into a truck and speed away.

What caused the death of the two thousand who lost their lives?

None of those who escaped mentioned lava, and it was clear that lava had had nothing to do with the deaths. Burning-hot gases and rock dust had done the damage. Many of those who escaped were frightfully burned, and all who saw the explosion talked about the black cloud swirling with red-hot sparks. It burst, they said, like an atom bomb to a height of seven

Mt. Lamington

miles or more and then came rushing down on them. If the estimate of three minutes in which to get away was right, that cloud of rock dust and hot gases came on at four miles a minute!

Spectacular as it was, the eruption of Mt. Lamington wasn't in any way special. There have been lots of explosions like it in the past. There will be lots like it in the future. It's what scientists call a hurricane blast type of explosion. It happens with volcanoes that seem to be dead. The eruption of Mt. Vesuvius in 79 A.D. was like that. The eruption of Mt. Pelée on May 8, 1902, was like that. Mt. Pelée was one of the worst. Perhaps it was the worst hurricane blast disaster of all time.

Mt. Pelée is a 4,000 foot mountain rising above St. Pierre, once the largest city in Martinique and one of the most important in the West Indies. Like Mt. Lamington and Vesuvius, Pelée was an old volcano. Everybody believed it to be dead or practically so. Some fifty years before, a little steam had, indeed, come out of a crevice at the top. But no one gave it any thought. Pelée looked so dead! Its slopes were grooved by ravines and gorges. The crater at the top was filled with blue lake water. It never occurred to anyone that the friendly, beautiful old mountain could cause death and destruction.

Then in the last week of April, 1902, the volcano began to act up. We know now that the signs of its waking were all warnings which the people of St. Pierre should have taken seriously. But they didn't. When now and again a column of smoke rose from the crevice near the crater and a light shower of ash fell on the city, a few people did get alarmed. But the rest looked on them as nervous folk who got panicky when there was nothing to be panicky about. To quiet them the authorities sent men up to investigate the crater. The men didn't find anything much to report. The water level of the lake had changed, they

St. Pierre before it was destroyed

said. As for the smoke, it seemed to be coming from a small cinder cone in the center of the lake.

Most of the 25,000 inhabitants were completely reassured. They went on preparing for the fourth of May when a big excursion up to the crater was being planned. Only the "panicky" ones continued to be alarmed. "Evacuate the city! Evacuate the city!" they kept repeating.

But the papers pooh-poohed the idea. "Mt. Pelée is no more to be feared by St. Pierre," one editor wrote, "than Vesuvius is feared by Naples. We confess that we cannot understand this panic. Where could one be better off than in St. Pierre?"

Apparently a good many people on Martinique felt the same way. For about 15,000 refugees from other parts of the island had fled to the city as being a safer place than their own.

On May fifth the volcano gave another warning, this time stronger. A stream of mud and lava came rolling down into the valley and buried some sugar works. Twenty-four people were killed. And still the Governor insisted there was no danger! Still he did all he could to keep the people from leaving the city. To show how little danger he thought there was, he himself took up his residence in St. Pierre. But now a good many folk were really alarmed. Although the scientists who were with the Governor kept declaring the volcano was behaving in a perfectly normal way, hundreds of people got out of the city.

Another day passed. Mt. Pelée looked angrier and angrier. On the seventh of the month an Italian ship was loading sugar at a dock in St. Pierre harbor. Her captain, a wary fellow, kept his weather eye on the volcano. Being from Italy, he had a healthy respect for smoking volcanoes, and though he had got only half his load aboard, he suddenly decided to leave.

The man whose sugar was being loaded started to

argue with him. "Finish the job!" he insisted. "Mt. Pelée threw out smoke and ashes before and no harm was done. Nothing will happen this time either!"

The captain shook his head. "I don't know anything about Mt. Pelée," he replied, "but if Vesuvius looked the way your volcano looks this morning, I'd get out of Naples. And I'm getting out of here!"

The shipper tried to prevent it. In a few minutes he had customs officers on board to forbid the captain to leave.

"Gentlemen," the captain said to them firmly, "I'm going to sail from this port in less than an hour. If you want to go ashore, now is your time to do it. If you stay with me, I assure you I will take you to France."

The men left and the vessel sailed away.

On the following day, the fatal eighth of May, seventeen ships lay anchored in St. Pierre harbor. Early in the morning another, the *Roraima,* came sailing in. Her decks were gray with the ash that had fallen on them out at sea, and yet the captain calmly anchored in the harbor. Unbelievable though it seems now, neither he nor any of the other captains sensed danger. All of them regarded the smoke and the constant muffled roaring as simply parts of a grand show.

In the early morning light the doomed city lay as though under a spell. Only the docks seemed to be alive. They swarmed with longshoremen loading the ships.

At about a quarter to eight there was a frightful explosion. A huge black cloud, burning hot and glowing a dull red in its inner folds, shot high into the air, then came leaping down the mountain. In another moment it had engulfed St. Pierre.

Sailors, frozen with horror, watched from the vessels as the smoke came rolling toward them. Aboard the *Roraima*, Second Engineer Evans had been looking at Mt. Pelée when the explosion came. He had seen the cloud shoot skyward, then leap down the mountain. Now as the glowing blackness advanced like a hurricane toward the harbor, he realized the danger. He heard the frantic captain shout to lift anchor, saw the sailors leap to the ropes, but knew it was too late. He fled to the safety of the engine room. A few seconds later the blast hit the *Roraima*. The vessel almost turned over. Bridge, masts, smokestacks—all were cut off in an instant, as though with a knife, and swept overboard. There was no fire in the cloud, but so intense was the smoke's heat that every pane of glass on the

ship broke. Every living thing the cloud touched
perished.

When it had passed and the engineer had groped
his way out through the darkness that surrounded
everything, only twenty-five of the sixty-eight crew
members were alive. Every one of those who had been
on deck was burned to death. The survivors tried to
put out the flames in mattresses and cushions. Neither

the wooden ship nor the load of lumber on deck had been set afire. The hot gases and ash passed over so quickly that only the most easily burned things were lit. These flames quickly spread and finished the destruction of sixteen of the eighteen vessels in the harbor.

On shore great fires swept everything in sight. But those main fires were lit not by the cloud of gases and ash. They resulted from the explosion of thousands of casks of rum stored in the city.

It was a scene of frightful desolation that met the survivors' eyes as they looked toward shore. Not a human being moved, not a human voice could be heard. The landings which a few moments before had swarmed with busy workers were strewn with dead bodies. The city itself lay as something dead. Only the tongues of flame that every moment increased and the smoke that still poured from Mt. Pelée were in motion. No one as yet knew that that first hurricane blast had burned or suffocated every human being but one in St. Pierre. That one was a prisoner deep down in the city jail.

8.

The Boiler Bursts

"Dead" volcanoes don't all erupt in exactly the same way, and the loss of life they cause isn't always due to a hurricane blast. When in 1883 Krakatoa blew up, tens of thousands of people lost their lives, not by burning or suffocation, but by drowning.

Krakatoa was a wooded island lying in a narrow strip of sea between Java and Sumatra. It had been built up to a height of 2,600 feet by the slow growth of several volcanoes that joined together. But it was not a large island and was not settled, though people often went there to pick wild fruit. Everybody knew Krakatoa to be a volcano. There were even some vents from which people sometimes saw steam and dust escaping. But as there had been no eruption for 200 years, everybody considered the volcano finished.

Inside it was not all peace and quiet, however. While the unsuspecting world went about its business, the biggest explosion of modern times was slowly building up. Scientists can't be sure what happened exactly. But everything leads them to believe that the eruption of Krakatoa was a steam explosion. The volcano exploded just like a boiler that bursts when the pressure of steam inside it becomes too great.

It is easy enough to see how it could happen. The surface rocks of Krakatoa had long been full of sea water—it had seeped in wherever there was a crack or crevice. That in itself was harmless. But combined with heat it meant trouble. Heat would cause the water in the rocks to turn to steam. The steam would get super-heated and expand. It would press more and more on the enclosing rock. Finally the rock would be unable to stand the strain any more and would give way and there would be a mighty explosion.

Explosion on the island of Krakatoa

In May, 1883, a rise of lava provided the heat necessary to start things going. Slowly the steam began to form. To the outside world it looked only as if Krakatoa had suddenly come alive and was erupting like any other volcano. And, indeed, that's exactly what it was doing at first. It erupted with loud noises that could be heard a hundred miles away. Smoke poured out to a height of seven miles. Dust fell three hundred miles away. For fourteen weeks Krakatoa kept that up, booming and fuming sometimes more, sometimes less. But all this was just the overture.

On Sunday, August 26, the island retired behind a cloud of black vapor. There were exploding sounds behind the curtain. Lightning kept ripping through the vapor. Stones dropped from the sky. The big explosions, however, were being reserved for the next day.

There were four of them, all very violent, and the third—the main explosion—was the most violent of all. There is nothing with which that third boom can be compared. It was said to be the loudest noise ever heard on this planet. Three thousand miles away on the island of Rodriguez a coast guard heard that sound and carefully noted down the time. It was four hours after the explosion. That's how long it took for the sound to travel a distance as far as from San Francisco to New York.

With that third mighty explosion the dust of Krakatoa shot higher up into the sky than anything from the earth had done since man was there to see it. Seventeen miles up it soared, perhaps more. And there it stayed. It was up so high that it couldn't come down at once. For the winds that blow at that level with a speed much greater than a hurricane seized the dust and swept it on. They swept it all around the earth. In thirteen days that cloud was back where it had

started from. But even then the dust didn't fall. The winds carried it on and on, around and around the earth—a dozen times perhaps. It was two full years before the last of Krakatoa sifted back to earth. The thick dust in the upper atmosphere shut out so much sunlight that the world's temperature dropped 13 degrees that year. All over the earth the sunsets were blood-red on account of the dust.

But these were the far-off effects. The explosion had at once disturbed the waves of the sea as well as those of the air, and on the low-lying shores bordering the Sunda Strait terrible things were happening. People had hardly got over the shock of the noise when a mountainous wave broke over the shore. There was neither time to flee nor place to escape to. In a few minutes the sea was sweeping far inland. Villages and towns crumbled. Before the water had returned to the sea, 36,000 people had been drowned.

Behind its pall of dust, Krakatoa had not yet stopped erupting; but it was running down and in a few days would be altogether still. The bursting of the boiler had been its last mighty effort. It had almost wiped the island off the earth. Where the volcano had risen to 2,600 feet, there was now just a hole. It was filled with water 900 feet deep!

9.

Tourist Attractions

The noise that Krakatoa made when the giant boiler exploded was a super-noise. But, as we have seen, there is plenty of racket any time a cone volcano is erupting hard. Dome volcanoes almost never put on that loud kind of display. They are the quiet sort. Just the same, their show is second to none—the eruptions of the domes are more beautiful, more interesting, and more varied than anything the cones can do. And the best part of it is that no terrible loss of life mars the spectacle, for dome volcanoes do less harm than any other kind.

There are domes in Iceland and Africa and other places, but to see them erupting at their best you have to go to Hawaii. The Hawaiian Islands, it will be remembered, are built by volcanoes. Only Hawaii, the largest and youngest of the islands, however, is still growing. It is there that we find the active volcanoes and also dead Mauna Kea, highest of all. Mauna Kea has finished its work of building Hawaii. Now Mauna Loa is carrying on that job. And while it builds up the island and extends its shoreline, it makes one of the best tourist attractions in the world. Anybody who has seen Mauna Loa at the height of eruption will say it's the grandest spectacle on earth.

Mauna Loa erupts pretty often—once every three years or so—and its fireworks are each time just about the same. Mild earthquakes come first. Soon after that the lava reaches the surface and the broad crater, which is five miles around, splits open. Then all along the line of the crack, fiery fountains of lava spring up. They go 300 to 500 feet up in the air and play very much like ordinary fountains. But the height of the sprays and the brilliant color and the changing lights—yellow as

Fire Pit of Kilauea

the lava goes up, red as it comes down—make a wonderful show, especially at night.

The famous Fire Pit of Kilauea is another grand tourist sight. It is only twenty-two miles from Mauna Loa crater and looks like an opening much lower down on Mauna Loa's side. But it's not a case of Parícutin and Zapicho. Kilauea is an independent volcano and older than Mauna Loa, whose child it looks to be.

The Hawaiians call Kilauea's crater *Halemauma.* That means "House of Everlasting Fire." But the fire can't always be seen—sometimes the lava is too far down in the crater. It was that way for twenty years

until recently when the crater filled up again. Now
people can again look down into a glowing cauldron
and see the boiling lava pool. Its surface is crusted with
a shiny black skin, webbed with glowing cracks. At
every crack the liquid boils and surges. Wherever the
crust is turning, the fresh lava glows brighter, and here
and there fountains spring up. At the margin, where
the crust bends and sinks, a row of little fiery fountains edges the pool. The wind catches the sprays and,
cooling them suddenly, sweeps them away as threads
of glass. Miles away people will find those threads
matted together in the crotch of a tree, or on a cliff

perhaps. "Oh, there is some of Pele's hair!" Hawaiians will say. Pele is the goddess of volcanoes.

One reason Hawaiian volcanoes can put on such a fountain display is that the Hawaiian lava is so thin. It has more iron in it and less silica than many other lavas, and that makes it much more watery. On this account, too, it has its own special way of flowing down a slope.

Commonly, Hawaiian lava doesn't go all the way down the mountain in the open where you can see it. As soon as it starts down, it sinks into a crevice and disappears. You think it's gone back down where it came from. But it has just gone into a tunnel. The lava flows on through that tunnel for thousands of feet. Then it comes out on the surface again, and you can see it the rest of the way.

Mauna Loa is honeycombed with tunnels, and more are being formed all the time. For they aren't ordinary caves such as those in which water runs through underground sometimes. They are caverns made by other lava flows.

The way they come about is this:

As lava flows along, it cools on the outside. The surface stiffens, slows up, forms a crust. On the inside, however, the flow stays hot and liquid. So most of the stream keeps flowing right along. It keeps flowing along *even after the spigot is turned off*; that is, even after the eruption stops. The result is that as the last of the hot lava flows through, it leaves an open tunnel behind it.

Hawaiian lava often travels miles and miles before it stops. Sometimes it has overflowed villages. Twice lava flows have threatened Hilo, the largest city on the island.

In 1881 a stream of lava traveled thirty-five miles and came to within half a mile of the city. The flow was so close that the inhabitants could feel the lava's heat. In a panic they sent to the princess of a neighboring island for help. Princess Kamahamena knew just what to do. She went out to the lava front, spoke some magic words, cut off a lock of her hair, and threw it into the lava. The magic was exactly right. Or maybe the lava was going to stop anyway. In any case the city was saved when the lava was just a few yards away.

In 1935 again a flow came toward Hilo. This time there was no princess and the authorities called in scientists instead. The scientists couldn't stop the lava from escaping, of course. But they knew that Mauna Loa's eruptions never last long. Perhaps, they thought, if they could make the lava take longer to travel the thirty-five miles to the city, the spigot would be turned off before the journey was finished.

They decided to try bombing. They would break open the roof of the tunnel through which the lava was flowing and force it out in the open. Then it would have to start out near the top again as a new tongue on a new path, but the first flow would stop dead because there was nothing to feed it. The thing would work just like a game of parcheesi when the player has to go back home and start all over again. If Mauna Loa stopped playing pretty soon, the lava might not have time to finish the game!

So a number of bombs were dropped. Some of them apparently hit just the right spot, for the tunnel broke down and the lava was forced into the open. It had to start out again as a new tongue. And long before that new tongue threatened the city, Mauna Loa stopped erupting.

Would the lava have stopped before reaching the city if no bombs had been dropped? We'll never know.

10.

On the Credit Side

Volcanoes are responsible for so much harm that it's only fair to give them credit where credit is due. And a surprising lot of credit is due. We don't hear very much about it—it's generally the bad points of volcanoes that get into the news. But the good points are there, and they weigh down the scales pretty heavily.

A good bit of the earth, as we have seen, is volcano-made. It is the volcanoes that are responsible for great land masses like the Deccan Plateau of India and our own Columbia River plateau. It is volcanoes that have built the Aleutians and Hawaii and Iceland and any number of smaller islands. It is volcanoes that have built the platforms for the coral isles.

But volcanoes have enriched the old as well as made the new. They have fertilized great tracts of worn-out soil. Java, for example, couldn't provide food for its many people if it weren't for the potash-rich soil that has been brought down from the slopes of the volcanoes. The volcanic dust that showers the slopes of Vesuvius and many other volcanoes is rich in potash, too. A heavy dusting of ash on the vineyards of Vesuvius may seem terrible when it happens. But in the following years the farmers find themselves gathering bigger harvests from the enriched land. It is with good reason that people take up farms near volcanoes even when it's dangerous to do so.

Cross section of a volcano

Some of the gases that volcanoes bring up from below are useful, too. Sulphur, for instance, changes into a solid and is deposited in the craters of volcanoes. In South America, New Zealand and Japan this sulphur is mined. It used to be mined in the crater at the top of Popocatepetl in Mexico. But now the job is considered too risky.

Sulphur is one of the elements that come up all the way to the surface with gases and magma. But there are other substances that drop by the wayside long before the gases, liquids and liquid rock have worked their way to the surface. Such are tin, tungsten, gold and other metals.

Few people realize how much we owe to the forces that make volcanoes. The fact is that without magma many metals wouldn't be within our reach at all. And others would be much deeper in the crust of the earth.

As everybody knows, most ore deposits are found only in certain places and in limited amounts. In the first place, that's because metals pretty much have to depend on magma movements to get them up. In the second place, it is because metals can be deposited only where conditions are just right for them. The heat, the pressure, and the rocks around must all be just what the metals need.

Sometimes the same conditions will suit two different metals. Then those two ores will be found together in the same mine. Thus lead and zinc are often found together. For they dissolve about as easily in the magma and separate out again about the same time. Mercury and antimony are found together for the same reason. As it happens, they come up most of the way with the magma and separate out near the surface. So it isn't surprising that they are found in new volcanic regions, where weathering has not yet worn away much of the rock. In the United States, mercury mines are all in the West, mostly in California.

Tungsten, beryllium, tin, and tantalum, on the other hand, are metals that don't come up very far with the magma. Indeed, they barely escape from the rock out of which they have been melted. They stay deep down

The great Cullinan diamond before it was cut

in the crust of the earth. When we find them at all, it is in the old volcanic regions where perhaps two miles of surface rocks have been worn away.

The most precious product of volcanoes is diamonds. As you probably know, they are carbon, like coal, but a very pure form. Chiefly they are found in the necks of old volcanoes—in the pipes, that is, through which the lava once came up. The volcanoes have weathered away and the necks are all that's left of them. Scientists think diamonds formed at a time when the lava in the necks was cooling and great pressure was exerted on the carbon.

All sorts of stones of a much less precious sort come out of volcanoes. Pumice is one. It looks like a brittle sponge and is the lightest stone in the world, so light that if you put it in water it will float. That's because it's filled with bubbles of gas. The lava got thrown out with such violence that the gas in it never had a chance to escape. It made a froth of hot stone. Before it could get out, the lava became solid.

Pumice makes a fine, soft powder which dentists use to clean teeth. Natural pumice isn't very common. So in recent years people have been making it out of volcanic glass, a type known as perlite. It's used in making lightweight plaster and cement mixtures.

Volcanic glass isn't being formed anywhere except in Hawaii today. But once it was made by lava flows in a number of places. Sometimes a whole flow would be glass, sometimes just the crust. Volcanic glass, or obsidian as it is called, is very beautiful and varied in color—black and gray and sometimes mahogany red. Indians used to prize obsidian as the very best material they had for arrowheads. In Mexico the Aztecs had almost a religious feeling about it. When they made sacrifices to their gods, they would use only knives of obsidian. In our own country the Mound Builders would walk all the way to the Yellowstone—a thousand miles—to get obsidian for their ceremonial knives. Nothing but obsidian would do.

Lapilli, the little stones that volcanoes throw up, have long been used in Italy and Germany. The beds of this volcanic gravel are easily dug and shaped. After drying out on the surface, the blocks become much harder and make excellent building materials.

Basalt

And even plain ordinary lava has its uses. When most lava flows harden, they become a rock called basalt. Wherever especially hard rock is needed, people turn to basalt. This volcanic rock is crushed to make roads and to add to cement mixtures. Before cement was invented, basalt used to be trimmed into cobbles for road paving. There are many basalt quarries in the eastern United States. Those of Paterson, New Jersey, are very well known. In the Connecticut Valley and near New Haven there are more great basalt quarries.

Once there were basalt quarries in the Palisades along the Hudson River. The Palisades are all that's left of a great lava sheet. They rise so straight and look like columns because the lava has cracks in it that go from top to bottom. It happened because the lava cooled from its surfaces and shrank. *Columnar jointing*, that kind of cracking is called. It makes for wonderful scenery. The Giants' Causeway in Ireland, the

Devil's Tower in Wyoming, the Columbia River Gorge, and the New Jersey Palisades all show the column effect. In some places such columnar rock is quarried. Along the Rhine there is a quarry where the columns are so slender and regular that they can be pried loose and piled like cord wood, to be used for fence posts.

Well, these are some of the good points of volcanoes. They add up, as you see, to quite a lot. Throw in the cones for beauty and the domes for display and you can't help coming to the conclusion that the good points outweigh the bad. Particularly, as the harm is so largely something which man could avoid if he took the volcanoes' warnings seriously and got out of their way in time.

Devil's Tower, Wyoming

11.
Old Faithful

Anyone who has been to Yellowstone Park has stopped to look at Old Faithful. It's thrilling to stand by the famous geyser and wait for it to shoot. It never disappoints you. Every 65 minutes a jet of hot water and steam squirts 140 feet or more into the air, plays for 4 minutes, then slowly sinks. Millions have marveled at Old Faithful. But not many have gone away understanding that this wild water-wonder is just a sideshow of vulcanism. The furnace that heats Old

Faithful is magma.

There was a time when some people thought all hot springs got their heat from hot rocks 'way deep in the earth's crust. "Just simple circulation," people said. "Cold water sinks through a crack and goes down and down. By and by it gets so far down that the hot rocks turn it to hot water. Hot water expands and gets lighter. Because it is lighter it rises again. And there's your hot spring."

The theory sounds all right, but the facts don't support it. Water just doesn't get down that far—at least not often enough to account for most of the hot springs. Underground streams do flow through caves that lie as much as 1,000 feet under the surface. But a thousand feet isn't far enough down.

Water does get down into mines—a Nevada mine had to close when it got down to 3,000 feet because the pumps couldn't handle all the water that came in. But 3,000 feet isn't deep enough for water to get really hot.

How much deeper does water go? Experience shows that it can't get much deeper—not often, anyway. There are very few cracks for water to sink through. As mines go deeper, open cavities become fewer and

Terrace pools at Hot Springs

fewer. Even the little spaces in the rock itself disappear as its joints are squeezed tighter. Some of the deepest mines are very dry. So there can't be many spaces where water can circulate freely 'way down. We have to conclude that from depth alone water can very seldom get hot enough to make a hot spring. Once in a while we do have to fall back on the simple circulation theory. But we do it only when a hot spring is very far from any volcanic activity and very far from the volcanic belts.

No, the hot water of most hot springs doesn't come from deep down in the earth. It rises from a very shallow depth. It gets its heat from magma that managed to get almost to the earth's surface but for some reason or other never did get all the way through. The hottest and most spectacular springs are always where volcanoes were active fairly recently—in Iceland, in New Zealand and in our own Yellowstone Park. Less hot ones, less spectacular ones are nearly all in the older volcanic regions. It's only a few that we can't account for that way.

For example, there are the hot springs of Arkansas. You might think, perhaps, that they had nothing to do with volcanoes because the region seems so far from any. Yet there is good reason to believe that once upon a time things weren't all peace and quiet there.

Arkansas also has mercury mines. That tells us something, too. Mercury, as we saw, is a metal that comes up with magma. It comes nearly all the way up, too. It deposits far from its original source. So it can't be so very many millions of years since there were volcanoes in Arkansas; otherwise, every trace of the mercury would have been worn away.

Indeed we find the necks of several volcanoes near Hot Springs, Arkansas. They have been very carefully studied, for one of them is America's only diamond deposit. Diamonds are found in the same way in South Africa in round bodies of volcanic rock called "diamond pipes." These are thought to be the tubes through which the lava came on its way to the surface to make the volcanoes.

But what makes a geyser? Why does the hot water

shoot up in that exciting fashion? Is it an explosion?

A very simple fact lies behind the shooting of a geyser. It is that water doesn't always boil at 212° F. The boiling point of water changes with the pressure. High up on a mountain the air pressure is less than at sea level. Up there it takes four or five minutes to boil a three-minute egg. That's because the water begins to boil at, say, 200° F. It can't get any hotter than that. But if you go down to Death Valley, it's just the other way around. Death Valley is below sea level. Water won't start boiling there till it reaches 213° or 214°. That little difference won't shorten the time you have to boil your egg, but the principle is clear—the more the pressure, the higher the temperature at which the water boils.

Now, let's see how this principle operates to make a geyser.

Down under the ground a geyser is a quite complicated affair. Scientists believe there are many feeding tubes, with branches here and swellings there, so that the whole thing looks like the roots of a clover plant. But to explain how a geyser works we don't need all that. We'll assume there is just one tube—the results will be the same whether we have branches or not.

Well, let's say Old Faithful has just gone down. As soon as the water seeps down and reaches the hot magma, it starts to heat. The feeding tube gets warmer and warmer. It gets warm all the way up because the water circulates—the cool water goes down, the warmer water comes up. By and by, all of it is good and hot. But still nothing happens. Though at the bottom of the narrow feeding tube the temperature is 'way above 212°, the water still doesn't boil. It can't boil so far down—under the pressure of all the water above it—till it gets to, say, 250°. So the water just heats and heats. But finally the column gets so hot that a big bubble of steam forms near the top and rises to the surface. When it breaks, it splashes a little water over the sides of the opening.

This is all that Old Faithful was waiting for. The moment that happens, the pressure changes all the way down the tube. For now there is less water to press down on the rest. The water boils at the bottom and up the tube and all of it instantly turns into shooting steam. In a moment the quiet pool of hot water becomes a rushing fountain. It rises high in the air, carrying the remaining water along with it into the sky. The whole feeding tube is emptied in a flash.

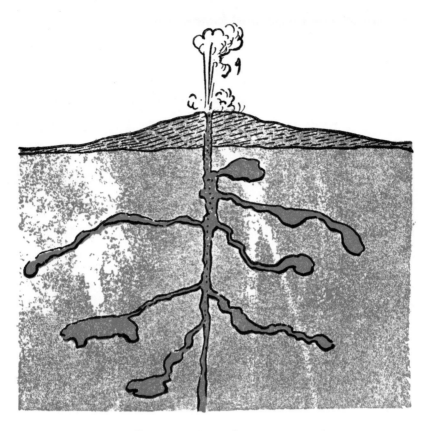

Cross section of a geyser

Now, if Old Faithful really had just one simple feeding tube, as we have assumed it did in order to make the explanation simpler, it wouldn't play like a fountain. It would just shoot up and come right down. It is the spreading roots of the feeding tube that let the geyser play for a while. Each far-spreading branch keeps adding its bit of hot water to this natural steam engine. That's what keeps the geyser up in the air.

How long is Old Faithful going to stay faithful?

Well, not forever, that's certain. Geysers are their own worst enemy. They bring on their own death. Every time the water in the feeding tubes has to be reheated, just that much heat is taken from the magma. The time must come when it takes longer for the water to heat because the magma isn't so hot any more. Already it is longer between Old Faithful's eruptions than it was some years ago when Yellowstone Park was first established. The day will come when Old Faithful shoots only once in twenty-four hours. The day will come when Old Faithful doesn't shoot at all.

12.

When the Earth Trembles

Geysers, we have said, are a sideshow of volcanoes. But volcanoes themselves are just a sideshow—they are but a symptom of something much more significant going on. That something is what keeps the continents up and the seas down. It is what builds the mountains over and over again. It is what wages endless war on the rain and snow and frost and wind that are forever working to plane the mountains down to the sea's level. That something is the mysterious force we call the crustal movements of the earth.

We feel those movements as a shaking of the ground beneath our feet. Sometimes the earthquake is violent. Sometimes it is hardly stronger than the passing of a truck on the highway. In some regions the earth shakes very often, in others an earthquake is a rare event. But all in all there is a great deal of shaking going on. Perhaps in a year there are as many as 150,000 tremors strong enough to be felt in places where people live. If we counted all, down to the smallest shake, there would be well over a million a year. No wonder that someone has said our earth has "a bad case of the shakes!"

It is a frightening thing, this quaking of the earth. We take firmness of the ground for granted. To feel it moving suddenly beneath our feet fills us with a strange uneasiness even when no damage is done. But when, without warning, a tremor rocks the foundations of buildings and sends them crashing to the earth, burying thousands beneath the ruins, we are filled with terror.

A volcano, after all, is something you can run away from. It gives you warning that it's going to erupt. But an earthquake doesn't warn before it strikes. It

The crustal movements of the earth

cannot be predicted for a certain day or month or year. You can't run away from it. It is upon you in an instant. In two or three minutes all is over and you are in the midst of ruin and death. Many, many times as many lives have been lost in earthquakes as in eruptions of volcanoes.

And yet people have grown a little tired of hearing about earthquakes. Newspapers don't seem to care about reporting them with all their horrors. But not because the disasters have grown less terrible. Far from it. The last fifty years have seen some of the very worst in history. In 1908 an earthquake in Messina,

Italy, took 50,000 lives. In 1920 one in China took 100,000. Japan counted 150,000 dead in an earthquake that hit Tokyo and Yokohama in 1923. And as recently as 1939, 40,000 were buried beneath the ruins of a Turkish city. In 1953, thousands more died in the same region.

Maybe the reason people have lost interest in earthquakes is that one is pretty much like another and just numbers of dead don't impress us any more. But let us see exactly what it is that happens in a violent earthquake. Let us see why so many lives are lost. And let us be fair and put the blame where the blame belongs. For the damage is not all the earthquake's fault. A great deal of it is our own. While it is true that we can't run away from an earthquake, there is much we can do to make the shaking of the earth a less fearful thing.

It doesn't matter whether we choose China or Chile, Italy, Japan, Turkey or New Zealand. Our earthquake will act just about the same. Nearly always it will start with a low rumbling noise—the earthquake sound. From moment to moment the sound will grow so that people who are near the worst part of the coming shock will distinctly hear it. But since the rumbling starts only perhaps half a minute before the quake itself, the sound can't really be called a warning. There is no time to do more than run out of the house. Often, and especially if the quake comes at night when people are asleep, there isn't time enough even for that.

Immediately afterward the ground shakes. Sometimes there is a series of backward and forward movements. Sometimes there is a wavelike motion. People standing on the ground feel seasick—while all about them walls start to tumble down. The earth movements last perhaps only two or three minutes. Yet in those two or three minutes of terror, panic and death a city can become a mass of ruin.

But here is the point. It doesn't have to. Just how bad the damage is depends on the kind of buildings in the city. If they are well-built structures with floors and ceilings properly braced—such as first-class modern skyscrapers with framework of steel—they will stand and the people inside will be safe. But if the houses are made of brick or stone and the roofs and floors and ceilings are not securely fastened to the walls, the structures will collapse like houses built of cards.

Then what happens is a nightmare. Scarcely do the survivors have time to get hold of themselves and begin the work of rescuing those in the ruins than smoke begins to rise. All over the city fires have broken out. How can they be put out? The streets are filled with debris. Wood and brick and stone and plaster are piled many feet high in every block. Fire engines are often buried or broken. If not, they can't get through the streets anyway, especially if it is an old city with narrow highways and byways. But in any case there will be very little water to fight fire with, for the pipes under and above the ground have been twisted and torn. The water pressure is gone, the fire hose can't be filled. And so fire eats its way through the city, house by house, street by street. There is no stopping the flames. Half the city goes, three quarters, sometimes all.

Such is an earthquake. Such is almost any earthquake that strikes a large city. But sometimes there are extra trimmings.

The city of Messina, for instance, is on the sea. A few minutes after the earthquake shock in Messina, the water withdrew from the beach and went far out to sea. But immediately afterward it came rolling back as an enormous wave that carried everything before it. Walls that started twenty-six feet above the level of the shore were swept away. And the wave went far beyond Messina itself. Villages so far away from the center of the shock that they hadn't been hurt by the quake at all were overwhelmed.

In Tokyo there was an even stranger event. The city was ruined and burning. In 136 different places fires had broken out within a half-hour of the quake, and from every quarter people were fleeing. Thousands had taken refuge on a large piece of open ground on a river bank. The place was so packed with human beings and their belongings that people could hardly move. And then fire began to close in on them on three sides. Sparks fell in showers, suffocating fumes choked them. But suddenly the people heard a sound that rose above all other sounds. The sky grew dark. They saw the black funnel of a tornado approaching, reaching out, turning this way and that. They saw the whirling wind lift the flames and set fire to everything in its way. When it had passed, the charred bodies of 35,000 human beings covered the ground.

Now, a great wave and a tornado are, of course, impossible to do anything about. But much of the death and destruction in an earthquake can be avoided. At Messina it was man's own fault, not Nature's, that almost all the houses were reduced to heaps of rubble. There was no need to find, time and time again, fifteen or more dead bodies buried one on top of another in a single small room on the ground floor. A Japanese scientist who was sent to the ruined city to find out the reasons for the great loss of life learned just how a city shouldn't be built.

Messina, he reported, had done all the wrong things. Many of the houses were built of river pebbles or bricks poorly cemented together. The people had put up house walls that were too high or too thin for their height. They had not fastened roofs and floors tightly to the supporting walls so that even when the walls themselves stood, the floors collapsed. They had built towers and high buildings close to low houses and then, when the taller structures fell, they destroyed their neighbors. And they had made the streets of Messina so narrow that the piles of debris completely blocked them.

But now let us forget man and his works for a moment and see what happens to the surface of the earth itself. We have said that the shaking of the earth is only an effect. It is a vibration that is set up by the sudden movement of the rocks in or near the crust of

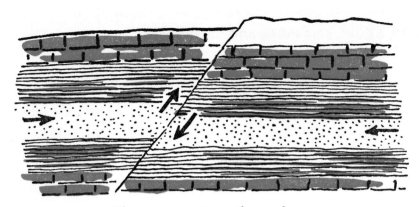

The movement on the surface

the earth. What results of that movement can we see? What happens to the surface when the rocks suddenly move?

One thing we know does *not* happen. The earth does not "yawn" as some storytellers have said. It doesn't gape open, swallowing whole villages and closing again as before. Occasionally a crack appears in the earth big enough for a man and his horse to tumble into. But such things seldom happen. The forces that cause the rocks to break are pushing forces, not pulling ones. They cannot pull rocks apart. They push them against each other, but if the surface bends upward it can crack.

The movement on the surface may be sideways, upward or downward. After a very severe earthquake we can trace the movement of the crust clearly. We can see the line along which the movement took place.

Sometimes we see other crustal changes. Mountains may be tilted or actually move higher in the air. Cliffs may be toppled. Slopes may slide down—yes, and bury villages. Domes may rise, cracks open. Settling may cause jets of water to spurt out and small sand craters to form.

Sometimes after a severe earthquake very great changes in level occur. But fortunately the greatest ones take place under the sea. In November, 1929, one of the greatest earthquakes of modern times took place under the Atlantic Ocean about 800 miles from New York City. The time and place of the quake and the center of the movement were exactly located. They were located because twelve Atlantic cables suddenly broke. The way they broke suggested that the support under them—the floor of the sea, that is—had suddenly dropped away. For each of the twelve cables was broken in several different places, and some of the breaks were 150 miles apart. It was clear that they had stretched when the bottom dropped and had broken by their own weight. In the end the scientists concluded that the ocean floor had dropped 25 feet.

Most earthquakes take place under the sea. So it is only sometimes that we can know what happens to the

Most earthquakes take place under the sea

crust when the earth trembles. Just the same we can often feel an effect of those undersea changes in the great waves that are set up.

We used to call such waves tidal waves. But we know now that they have nothing to do with tides and we call them by the Japanese name *tsunami*. Tsunami are not always started by an earthquake. They may also be started by underwater volcanoes. When Krakatoa exploded, it started up such a wave, you'll recall. But most tsunami are set up by earthquakes. Tsunami travel at a terrific pace—hundreds of miles an hour, it is said. They don't do any harm so long as they are out to sea. In fact, ships may not even know when they are riding tsunami. It is only when the wave reaches land that it is dangerous. As it nears the shore, the wave sucks water and boats away from the beach. Then it comes crashing in, bringing the boats back. Often the water sweeps far over the land where it may leave the boats stranded. At the same time it destroys whatever is in its path. Catching up people, it may fling them high up on the land.

The most surprising thing about tsunami is that the damage they do is so far from their starting point. Tsunami travel hundreds, even thousands of miles. The one started by the quake that broke the Atlantic cables damaged ships in Newfoundland, where the quake wasn't even felt. More recently fifteen-foot waves washed up on the Hawaiian shore. They killed people and washed away boats and homes. And yet those tsunami were started by a quake that took place near the Aleutian Islands!

13.

Up and Down and to the Side

A couple of hundred years ago people would have been astonished to learn that most earthquakes strike under the floor of the sea. They would have opened their eyes wide to hear that most aren't even felt by man because they are either too far from places where people live or too weak to register on human beings. Our ancestors probably wouldn't have believed it—because there were no sensitive instruments then to prove it.

Now we have instruments that feel and record the slightest trembling of the earth. We call them *seismographs*. The name comes from *seismos*, which is the Greek word for "earthquake." And the scientists who work with these instruments and study earthquakes are called *seismologists*—people who study earthquakes.

After a while we are going to see just how the seismographs and seismologists work. But for the moment we'll stop to say only that between them they are able to determine several important things. They can determine the exact center of the earthquake—that is, how far down in the earth the rock movement occurs. They can determine the *epicenter*—that is, the place on the surface of the earth that is just above the center of the earthquake. And they can determine how strong the movement is.

"But," you might ask at this point, "why do the rocks move at all? What causes the sudden movement in the crust that sets up the vibrations we call earthquakes?"

To understand that, you will have to stop thinking of rocks as being absolutely rigid. Rock layers in the earth's crust are elastic. Rock will bend. It is being bent all the time by the great pressures that are ex-

Deep earthquake without surface break

erted on it. Sometimes it is bent so slowly and over such long periods of time that it buckles, or warps, or folds. But sometimes strain is added to strain and at last there comes a moment when the rock can't take any more. Then, like the camel's back that couldn't bear the weight of one last straw, the rock snaps and takes up a new position to relieve the strain. Sometimes it is a rock layer near the surface of the earth that snaps. Sometimes it is rock much farther down. The breaks seldom come up all the way to the top, but on the inside the crust is crisscrossed with them.

So far as our cities are concerned, it is the shallower earthquakes that we have to worry about—those that start from five to twenty miles below. For it is they that hit the surface hardest. It is they that actually appear on top in the form of cracks and ground shifts. Also they are the most frequent kind. Seldom do fractures in the rock start lower than twenty miles down. When they do, they generally don't reach the top with enough force to do damage. Sometimes it does happen, but not so often. In 1939 an earthquake that started 43 miles below the surface struck near Chillan in Chile, did a lot of damage, and caused the death of 25,000 people.

We call anything below twenty miles a *deep-focus* or Plutonic earthquake. There is much about such earthquakes that we don't understand, especially those that center hundreds of miles below the surface.

One earthquake is said to have had its center 435 miles down—well over a tenth of the way to the center of the earth. Scientists can't all bring themselves to accept that figure. And it's no wonder! For it's hard to imagine how rock which at that level must be liquid or at least plastic can at the same time be so brittle that it will break suddenly and start the jiggles that are an earthquake.

Seismologists tried for years to explain the deep-focus earthquakes by calling them reflections of shallower earthquakes. But everybody has now come to agree that there really are earthquakes 'way down in the earth. In 1928 an earthquake that was felt in Japan was found to have started 254 miles under the Pacific Ocean floor. Most scientists accept that. In fact, they have even come to believe that it is the deep-focus earthquakes that are most important in lifting the mountains and keeping the continents high.

Once people thought all earthquakes were caused by volcanoes, or, at least, were tied up with them in some way. And that isn't at all strange. For doesn't the earth shake every time a volcano erupts—before, during and after? And aren't most of the earthquakes right in the same regions where most of the volcanoes are?

We know better now. We know that volcanic earthquakes are in a small class by themselves. They have nothing to do with the ordinary *tectonic* or "building" earthquakes. Volcanic earthquakes are connected with movements of magma under the crust and are closely related to the eruption of the volcano. They may be caused by explosions in a crater. They may be due to a break in the rock near the volcano. Or they may be the result of just the pushing of gases in lava.

Such earthquakes are all very local and extremely shallow. They may be quite strong close to the volcano, but their strength quickly dies a very little way off. A volcanic earthquake sometimes won't even be felt by a sensitive seismograph just a few miles away. And this shows just how very shallow the quake is. For a tectonic earthquake, so slight that it could scarcely be felt by people on the ground right above the center, would be recorded on a delicate seismograph a thousand miles away.

It is the tectonic earthquakes that interest us most because it is they that affect us most. We see three kinds of them active in our own country. One kind is at work on our West Coast, an area, you will recall, that is part of the mountain-making belt around the Pacific. There a crumpling of the rocks is going on all around the edges of the ocean. Perhaps this is because the continents, as we have said before, may be sliding over against the stronger ocean basin. But be this as it may, slowly, over millions of years, mountain-high rock ripples are forming. The San Francisco earthquake of 1906 and a whole series of other earthquakes were all part of this process.

How many thousands of earthquakes does it take to build a mountain? We don't know. But we do know that Nature isn't in any hurry. We do know that every

little earthquake helps. California heights have actually been measured after various earthquakes and found to be higher. And the same thing is true elsewhere. Scientists have figured out that not far from Tokyo, four earthquakes raised the land 45 feet in a period of centuries. In Alaska after a series of quakes in 1899 a rise of 50 feet occurred all in one jump.

Many earthquakes in California take place along a line that is called the San Andreas Rift or the San Andreas Fault. It is a line of weakness in the earth's crust where the rock has cracked and moved and where earthquakes have taken place again and again over countless years. The Rift is so well known that everybody calls it by name. "There goes the San Andreas Rift slipping again!" Californians say when they see in the paper that there has been another shock.

This San Andreas crack is the longest one we know anywhere. It runs north and south for a distance of over 600 miles. At the north end it loses itself in the sea, and at the south end in the Colorado Desert. You can follow the Rift very clearly from the air. In places it shows as a chain of troughs and ridges. In other places you can see a cliff anywhere from a few feet to a hundred feet high. Some places show signs that there has been sideways movement along the Fault as well. At the time of the San Francisco quake a part of the Fault broke for a distance of 270 miles and the side nearest to the coast traveled to the northwest. At one point the shift measures 21 feet.

The Rift is so old that some of the signs of movement are almost worn away. But among the very oldest are some that show bigger shifts of the surface than any of the recent ones. Two sides of a gully, for example, are separated by as much as 150 feet. Does it mean that in recent times California hasn't seen any really great movement along the San Andreas Rift? Or does it mean that what looks like one big movement is in fact a merger? Perhaps there never was any big push. Perhaps just a lot of little ones added up to what seems like a really big movement. We don't know. There is so much about earthquakes that we don't know.

In the lower Mississippi Valley we have a different kind of tectonic earthquake. There every time there is an earthquake the crust of the earth sinks. We can explain it in only one way. The muddy Mississippi brings down a great deal of sediment. Year by year it piles up that sediment till the earth's crust can't stand up under the weight. So it adjusts by sinking a little.

In New England and New York State we have exactly the opposite effect. There the movement is up, not down. That region is making up for what happened to it in the Ice Age. Twenty thousand years ago an ice sheet a mile thick covered New England and New York and pressed the area down. Now that the ice has gone, the land is slowly coming back to normal. The greatest rise now is in the north where the ice stayed longest and lay thickest. All the crustal rebound hasn't happened yet—the area still isn't quite back to where it was when the ice was there. But every few years there is a jerk. Each New Hampshire earthquake we read about is another of those little jumps.

And now we come to the final question. We have

said that earthquakes are vibrations set up by the snapping of rock in the crust of the earth or deep down below. We have said that the rocks snap because they can't stand the strains caused by the pressure. Now we must ask: What causes the pressure? What starts the mountain-building process in which earthquakes play a part?

We have to admit at once that we don't know. We know little pieces of the answer. But we don't know how to put them together and, besides, a good many of the bits are missing.

We know, for instance, that mountains are being made along the weak places in the crust. We know that volcanoes break through in those weak places. We know that earthquakes occur in the same places. We know that both of them have a part in building up the land. But we don't know what causes the magma to rise. And we don't know what causes the upward pushing against the rocks. Perhaps it is the same thing in both cases. Perhaps radioactive elements that give off heat may have something to do with it. Perhaps an increase in heat due to some other cause starts the rock down in the earth flowing and pushing against the rock above.

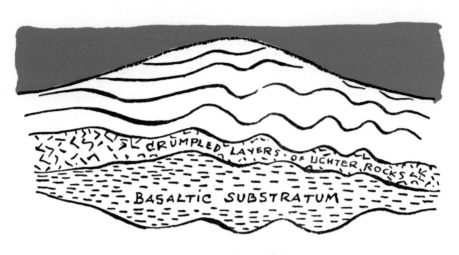

Mountains rising from their roots

We don't know. We can't get down into the earth to see what is happening. We can only watch what is taking place on top and reason from that. Weights are piling up in some places and causing land to sink. The rock base under Greenland, for instance, has been bent into a saucer shape because of the weight of ice. Other places are rising because a weight has been lifted. New England is rising. Scandinavia is rising half an inch a year. In other places, again, mountains are being worn down at the top by rain and wind and snow and frost. But at the same time, as if to make up for the loss, the mountains are rising from their roots.

We live on an ever-changing planet. As long as there

is heat left inside the earth it will always be so. Up on the moon there are no changes, for the moon is a cold, dead world. But the earth is very far from that state yet. As long as men live on earth, and probably long after they are gone, earthquakes will play their part in making geography ever new. The high places of the earth will be worn down, and their waste will fill up the low places. The solid rocks of the crust will be pushed down in some spots and buoyed up in others. Strains will arise. Breaks will come to release the strains. Rocks will spring up or drop down—and time and again the earth will shake.

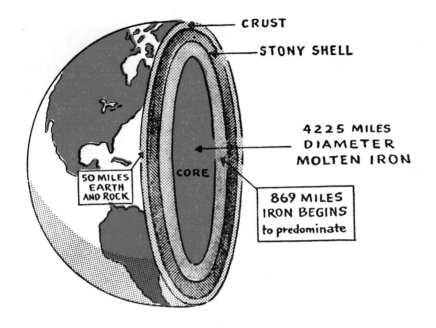

CRUST

STONY SHELL

4225 MILES
DIAMETER
MOLTEN IRON

CORE

50 MILES
EARTH
AND ROCK

869 MILES
IRON BEGINS
to predominate

14.

Messages from Below

We are so used to scientific wonders that when we first hear there is an instrument that detects and measures the trembling of the earth we just take it as a matter of course. But when we stop to think about it, isn't it an amazing thing? How can something standing on the earth tell us how fast and in what direction the earth itself moves? We cannot detect motion as such. We can tell a thing is moving only in relation to something that is standing still or moving at a different speed.

If you are on a train, you can tell you are moving because you look out of the window and see that houses and trees and telegraph poles are left behind you. But if you close your eyes, you will think you are standing still. That's because you and the train are moving together. Now, any instrument standing on the earth must move along with the earth. So how can it tell us in what direction and how fast the earth itself is moving? There is nothing to compare the motion with.

It would seem that in order to make a record of the shaking of the earth—or of the wiggles of something that is resting on the ground—we would have to hook our instrument up in the sky somehow so that the instrument itself would stand still. Funny as that sounds, it is exactly what scientists have done. They have suspended their recording instrument from a wire!

"Yes, but the wire is still on the earth," you say. "So how does that help?"

It helps because of a certain law which we call *inertia*. It is a very simple law and one we see operating every day. All it means is laziness. You have heard about the boy who was very lazy but at the same time was a wonderful worker because when he once got started he was too lazy to stop? Well, that's inertia. When we are up, we don't want to go to bed, and when we are in bed, we don't want to get up.

Anybody who has been in an automobile has experienced the effects of inertia. The car starts suddenly and you fall back in your seat. Why? Because your body doesn't want to start moving. It doesn't respond instantly to the movement of the car and gets left behind. Or the car stops suddenly and you are thrown forward. Why? Because your body doesn't want to stop moving. It doesn't respond instantly to the stopping of the car and keeps right on going.

Now, this principle is what makes it possible for us to record the movements of the earth. It is by taking advantage of inertia that the seismograph records the shaking of the earth.

This is not a new idea. Back in the year 132 A.D. a Chinese by the name of Chang Heng, Director of the Bureau of Almanac and History, invented a seismoscope. It didn't look very much like our seismograph and it didn't do as good a job, but it was really built on the same principle.

Chang Heng's instrument was a covered copper jar

shaped like a barrel and about three feet across. On the
outside of this jar, eight dragons' heads were set equal
distances apart, each dragon's head with a ball in its
mouth. Around the base of the jar sat eight frogs.
Each held its mouth wide open right under a dragon's
head as if ready to catch the ball if the dragon should
let it drop. And every time there was an earthquake
a ball did fall right into a frog's mouth. For inside the
jar, a pillar-like pendulum was suspended from the
cover. When the earth shook, the swaying pillar inside
would strike the back of one of the dragons and knock
the ball out of its mouth. This showed two things:
that there had been an earthquake and the direction in
which it had taken place.

Our seismograph today isn't nearly so handsome, but it makes a better record. Very simply it works like this:

A wire is suspended from a bar. At the end of the wire a weight is hung and to the weight a recording needle is attached. The needle just touches a drum of paper turned by clockwork. The drum itself stands on a base of concrete that goes right on down to bedrock. When the earth shakes, the concrete base moves with it. Every sideways movement pushes the drum back and forth under the needle attached to the weight, which on account of inertia is standing still. And a jiggly line is produced. It is the handwriting of the earthquake, a wireless message from below.

That is the way a seismograph works. But if you were looking at one while it was recording, you would say it worked just the opposite way. You would say the needle and the weight and the wire were moving and the drum and the concrete base were standing still. It would seem so to you because you, too, would be moving along with the earth. In just the same way when you are on a ship that is leaving a pier, it will seem to you that the pier is moving and you are standing still.

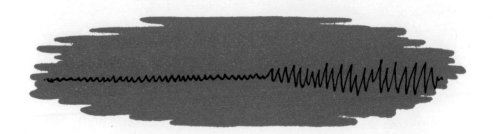

A seismograph is actually a more complicated instrument than we have described. For instance, there is a special arrangement that makes the movement bigger so that a push of the drum that is only a fraction of an inch is magnified into a swing of three or four inches. And the new seismographs don't have a needle writing down the jiggles of the earth at all, but use a beam of light instead. The light is reflected from a delicately hung mirror onto a sheet of photographic paper. Such a seismograph has to be kept in a dark cellar, and, of course, the seismologist doesn't even know that an earthquake in some far-off place has occurred until he has taken the paper off and developed it.

We say that a seismograph records the movements of the earth's crust. But what exactly do the marks on the drum represent?

When you break a wire spring in two, the actual break is over in an instant. Still, the wire spring goes, "Zing-g-g!" as it breaks and vibrates back and forth for several seconds or a minute. The earthquake break is also over in an instant. And the broken rock, like the broken spring, keeps on vibrating a few seconds or minutes. Actually the quiver that goes through the earth is a double quiver. One quiver pushes the earth ahead of it. The other twists or shakes the earth from side to side.

We call the first wave a P-wave. Its movement is like the movement that goes through a long freight train when the engine gives a starting jerk on the first car—push-pull. The P-waves go through rocks very fast, something like five miles a second. It takes only about twenty minutes for a P-wave to get all the way to the other side of the earth.

The second wave starts out at the same time, but it gives a sideways yank to the rock particles. It is like the wave that travels along a jump rope when you move your end sideways. We call this a *shear* or an S-wave. It travels much more slowly than a P-wave, only about three miles a second. So the two waves

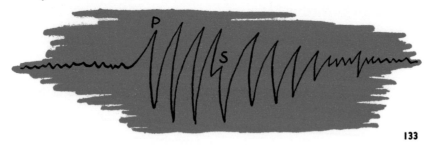

don't get to the seismograph at the same time. And that is very significant for us because the difference in arrival time tells how far away the earthquake happened.

It's just as with thunder and lightning. We see the lightning first and hear the thunder afterward. That's because light travels faster than sound. We can tell how far away the storm is by the difference in time between lightning and thunder. If the two come close together, then the storm is near. If the thunder takes a long time to reach us, the storm is far away.

So with the P- and S-waves. Let's say the S-wave comes in two seconds after the P-wave. Then we know that the earthquake was very close—15 miles away. If the two waves were six seconds apart, we would know that the earthquake was 45 miles away. If they were 600 seconds apart—ten minutes, that is—we would know that the center of the earthquake was 4,500 miles away.

Of course, distance alone doesn't tell the seismologist very much. Just by knowing how far away an earthquake occurred doesn't tell him where it happened. Because it might be north, east, south, or west, or at any point in between. He has to get in touch with two other observatories and find out what their records show. When he knows how far the earthquake was from them, he draws a circle around each city, using the distance of the quake from that city as a radius. The three circles intersect at one point only. And that's where the quake was.

A seismologist doesn't get excited when he sees that his instrument has recorded a strong earthquake. He doesn't hurry for reports from other observatories to find out where the quake was so he can tell a waiting world about it. He knows that most likely the earthquake that looks so exciting on paper happened in some far-off place under the sea and will never be heard of again. He knows that damaging earthquakes are rare.

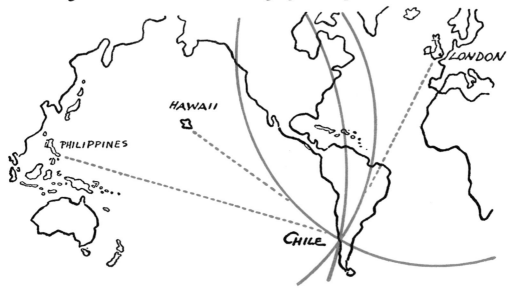

In any case, the world isn't waiting for him. If damage is done, the news will be on the wires long before he gets his circles drawn and the quake located. And if no damage is done, nobody is going to be interested.

Nobody except seismologists, that is. Of them he can always be sure. Seismologists feel there is a great deal that earthquake wave pictures have to teach us besides how strong and deep down and far away the earthquakes are. And, indeed, it is seismographs that have given us the most reliable picture of the inside of the earth.

You will remember that at the time we were discussing how volcanoes work, we said that some of the earthquake waves pass through the first 1,800 miles of the earth as though it was a solid. It is the S-waves that gave us that information. Shear waves, the sideways moving waves, don't go through a liquid. But they do pass almost halfway to the center of the earth. After that they are lost. We can only suppose that below 1,800 miles the rocks lose their stony solidity. Perhaps they become a glassy liquid that is unable to pass along shearing earthquake waves.

The seismograph is the eyes and ears of anyone who wants to know what is going on inside the earth. Some-

times our interest in what's going on is purely scientific. Sometimes there is a very practical reason for knowing. In the matter of oil the reason is very practical. Oil prospecting has become the most important use for the seismograph.

But can a seismograph really tell where oil is trapped in the rock?

No, it can't. But it can do the next best thing. It can show where there is a trap. Oil prospectors have found that oil rises and collects in the high places, or domes, of rock layers. A seismograph can find out just how far down in the earth such a dome is and so help decide where to drill for oil.

The seismograph can do that because certain earthquake waves are reflected, or echoed, back to the surface by some rock layers. What prospectors do is make an artificial earthquake. They dig a hole and shoot off a charge of dynamite. The waves of that little handmade earthquake travel in all directions like the waves in a pond when you throw a stone in. Some also go down into the earth and are reflected back in part from a rock layer under the ground.

The seismograph first gets a quiver from the wave that came directly to it along the surface of the ground. A few moments later it gets a second quiver. That second quiver is the echo. The wave that went down into the crust hit the top of a reflecting layer and came back up. The journey of the wave that went down and was reflected back was a good deal longer than the route of the surface wave. So naturally it arrived later. The whole point is in how much later. The difference in time tells how deep down in the earth the reflecting layer of rock is.

It is in the Gulf States that seismographs are especially useful in this way. There the rock layers are buried so deep that not a single place can be found where the bedrock sticks out above the ground. The land is all just a flat plain covered with a deep blanket of mud and sand. The seismographs show up what is under the ground. They make it possible to map rock domes just as though they were above ground. If not for the seismographs a great deal of labor and expense would have to go into drilling holes to find where the oil traps are.

15.

Getting Ready for the Next One

Earthquakes differ so much in strength that to say this many shocks occur here and that many there doesn't mean very much. But if we measure how severe the various quakes are, what do we find?

We find that 80 percent of earthquake energy takes place in the belt right around the Pacific. Another 15 percent occurs in a belt that starts in Mexico, goes across the West Indies to the Mediterranean and Central Europe, then swings over through Asia Minor,

India, and the East Indies to meet the first belt in the South Pacific. That leaves 5 percent of earthquake energy for the rest of the world!

We are in luck. Except for the West Coast, the United States is pretty well set. And yet that 5 percent of earthquake energy in which we share has given us plenty of shocks. In the years 1811 and 1812 a whole series of earthquakes occurred near where the Ohio and Mississippi Rivers join. Probably this was the worst series of quakes ever to hit the United States. Fortunately at that time the valley wasn't thickly settled. At New Madrid, Missouri, the nearest town, people were still living in log cabins; so no lives were lost and little damage was done to property. But the region itself was greatly changed. Some areas rose, others sank. A forest was flooded and drowned. Reelfoot Lake in Tennessee formed. In the Mississippi, islands sank and banks caved in.

Some scientists were in Kentucky on February 7, 1812, when the worst of six shocks occurred. Audubon, the naturalist for whom our bird societies are named, was riding horseback at the time and he reported that "the ground rose and fell in successive furrows like the ruffled waters of a lake. The earth waved

Audubon was riding horseback at the time

like a field of corn before the breeze."

The shocks were certainly severe. Three of them were felt as far away as the Atlantic coast. It is said that in Boston, 1,100 miles away, clocks stopped and a church bell rang of its own accord, while down in Virginia and the Carolinas plaster cracked. Doors and windows rattled in Washington, 800 miles away. In Cincinnati, 400 miles away, chimneys were thrown down. One person in Kentucky kept a careful record of the shocks that occurred in this series from December 16, 1811, to March 15 in the following year. There were 1,874 of them, eight violent and ten very severe!

All About Volcanoes and Earthquakes

On August 31, 1886, Charleston, South Carolina, and the nearby area suffered the worst quake ever to hit the Atlantic Coast—at least in historic times. Fortunately only forty people lost their lives. Considering how severe the earthquake was, very little damage was done. In the city itself only something over 100 buildings were destroyed and nearly all the brick ones damaged. The earthquake disturbed an area of 2,800,000 square miles. The shock was felt all the way from Canada to the Gulf of Mexico. As far as Milwaukee, Wisconsin, windows were reported to have been broken by that quake.

New Madrid and Charleston were our worst in the East. But that 5 percent in which we share has pretty well spread through the country. Boulder Dam, for example, across the Colorado River has quite an earthquake problem. In 1937 alone, 143 shocks were felt in the area right around the dam. Chicago and New York have both had shocks, though none serious, while Boston in 1755 had quite a severe one. New England is always having quakes. Montana, Utah and Nevada have all had destructive ones. All the West Coast states have had quakes and many of the rest.

What are the prospects? Is it possible that one of

Boulder Dam

our large cities not on the West Coast will be struck some day by a serious earthquake as San Francisco was?

We don't know. Nobody can say. But there is always a possibility. Remember that in 1929 one of the severest earthquakes of modern times took place under the Atlantic Ocean only 800 miles away from New York.

Can we do anything about it?

We certainly can't run away. Nor is it necessary to. All we have to do is take some earthquake lessons to heart. Messina and Tokyo and San Francisco have all taught us one thing we ought to do—make our buildings earthquake-proof. A good guide to that is to imagine that some giant like Paul Bunyan could pick up a house or apartment building and turn it upside down. Would the roof fall off and all the floors drop out till he was left holding nothing but a cellar? Or would it hold together like a welded steel skyscraper with only a few loose bricks of the chimney dropping off? If so, it is a safe building.

Then there is the matter of fire. We have learned over and over again that the fire which follows a quake is a bigger destroyer of life and property than the earthquake itself. In the San Francisco earthquake only 5 percent of the damage to property was due to the quake. It was fire that destroyed the city. The water mains in many places were broken, the pressure was gone, and soon the fire was out of control. For three days the fire raged. Buildings in the path of the fire were finally dynamited to rob the flames of fuel, and at last rain fell.

San Francisco may suffer another earthquake, but never again will it have such a fire. Precautions have been taken. Several pipe lines, far from one another, have been set up. An entirely separate fire system has been installed that will supply water from a second reservoir or even fill fire hose with sea water. Besides

In the San Francisco earthquake, fire destroyed the city

this, a whole series of water cisterns has been placed underground in various parts of the city. People in San Francisco can know that everything possible has been done to protect their city from fire.

Other cities can profit by San Francisco's example. It is better to shut the stable door before the horse is stolen. It is wiser to be prepared for earthquakes than to say, "It can't happen here." We can't wait till the seismologists predict an earthquake will strike our city. It's going to be a very long time before anybody can predict an earthquake.

All About Volcanoes and Earthquakes

Predicting eruptions has got a lot farther. And that's natural. Volcanoes stand out, they can be watched. Of course, we can't tell where a new one will pop up. No one could have foreseen that Dionisio Polido would one day be the unhappy owner of a baby volcano. But we generally can predict when a volcano is going to give trouble.

Vulcanologists and seismologists have made a team to guard the world against unexpected eruptions and to warn people who live near volcanoes when danger approaches. The teamwork still isn't foolproof—the loss of life when Mt. Lamington exploded in 1951 is evidence of that. But progress is being made. In 1914 scientists warned the people on the island of Sakura-jima, Japan, that their volcano was getting ready to erupt. The entire population—23,500 people—were immediately made to move from the island, and when the great explosion came, not an islander was lost.

We are moving ahead. We are beginning to understand how this restless earth of ours renews its crust and what we must do to make it a painless process for man. Knowing it's largely up to us, we can look ahead with confidence. The time will surely come when volcanoes will not be dreaded and when earthquakes will break only vases and plates. We can't stop the mountains from being made. Nor do we want to. But we can cooperate. We can keep ourselves from getting hurt while our geography is being renewed.

Index

Index